TALKING
WITH
ANGELS

Strive to Live your Life iN
Integrity, LOVE, & TRuth...
Many Blessings,
RicH & DEE Tuminello

TALKING
WITH
ANGELS

RICHARD & DENISE TUMINELLO

Outskirts Press, Inc.
Denver, Colorado

Outskirts Press, Inc.
http://www.outskirtspress.com

ISBN: 978-1-4327-4431-1

Outskirts Press and the "OP" logo are trademarks belonging to Outskirts Press, Inc.
PRINTED IN THE UNITED STATES OF AMERICA

Dedication

We would like to dedicate this book to our children Christopher, Richard, and Christine. We are so very thankful we were blessed with their most beautiful spirits and souls, and love them with all of our hearts. Also to our Fathers, Domino Tuminello and George Hunter who no longer walk on the Earth plane, but are there to guide us in spirit always. Our love for you is everlasting. "As Above So Below"

Table of Contents

Introduction.. ix

Prologue.. xi

Part One

1 My First Visit to The Monroe Institute 3

2 First Past Life 9

3 Akashic Records... 13

4 After Gateway... 15

5 Remote Viewing Class 21

6 Taking Off for the First Time.. 23

7 Transmuting Thoughts to God.. 29

8 The Center 31

9 Second Retrieval... 35

10 The Library.. 41

11 Is this Confirmation that it is All Real? 47

12 Standstill 49

13 Jerry.. 55

14 Galactic Federation.. 59

15 Exploring with the Kids... 63

16 Letter from Jerry about my Journeys 67

17 The Cosmos... 71

18 Back to the Federation 75

19 Nothing Works 81

20 Mount Rushmore 83

21 Healing Temple 87

22 Brothers 91

23 Travel Without Hemi-Sync 97

24 Out of Phase 103

25 Apple Pie 107

26 Sparkie 111

27 Pirates 115

28 Dad 119

29 Ladies Shoes 121

30 The Beige Blanket 127

31 Eyes of an Angel 129

32 Manifestation and Creation² 133

33 Dee 137

Part Two

34 Are They Listening? 147

35 Michael 153

36 Metatron 157

37 Merging 159

38 Obsidian Tears 165

39 Light Being 171

40 Yeshuah 175

41 Past Lives with Dee 179

42 The Angel Team.............................187
43 A Day with the Angels.....................195
44 Healing.....................................197
45 Grounding..................................203
46 Overload...................................209
47 Lily Dale..................................213
48 New Entities...............................223
49 Sedona.....................................229
50 Changes....................................237
51 Saturday...................................245
52 The Angels Came to Play....................249
53 Starman....................................253
54 A Journey of Light.........................263
55 Raising My Level...........................267
56 A Trip Back to the Ether...................271
57 Light and Darkness.........................273
58 Twin Flames................................279
59 Sedona II..................................281
60 The Triple Crown...........................285
61 Michael and My Heart.......................293
62 Twenty Seconds.............................299
63 Costumes...................................303
64 Different Levels...........................305
65 Sleepless Nights...........................311
66 Church Visit...............................315
67 One Soul...................................317

68 Amah 319

69 Dee's Illness 321

70 Healing Hearts 325

71 Cozumel 331

72 The Field 337

73 Dad Again 339

74 New Teachings 343

Epilogue 353

Acknowledgement 363

INTRODUCTION

This book is presented in Two Parts as my journey to a whole new life and one that I never knew existed prior to the last couple of years. Part One covers my studies at The Monroe Institute (TMI) and my continuation of this wonderful journey on my own. Part Two covers my communication with Angels. A journey that I am on and don't really know where it will end.

My story is a bit different than most adventures that I have read about. It begins at TMI but then takes off in a completely different direction, one that I have not heard about previously happening to anyone, although I do not feel that I have been the only person to experience these things here on Earth. I have to say at the outset that if these experiences did not happen to me, I would be very doubtful of them actually happening to anyone. But, like all events that are relayed by individuals, one has to experience them for themselves before they can know that they *actually occurred.*

I started out on this journey as a complete novice when it came to other states of consciousness. However, I quickly was able to surpass anything that I would have thought to be possible on this Earth Plane. After a quick start at TMI I continued my journeys by myself. I was able to begin retrievals on my own and then went to the "Library" in the Ether for additional experiences that took me onto my next level of communication with Angels. You see, I am now communicating with Angels and they are communicating with me in a very real sense. For the past year I have been working with Angels and accomplished two things: (a) they have raised my own personal vibrational level from the Earth Plane to a much higher level which allows me to communicate with them; and (b) they enabled me to actively assist someone else in a healing process on their physical body.

During the process I have been able to learn much about the other side of the veil and have been able to do things that I would have never thought possible before. You see, the Angels that are working with my wife, Denise, and I not only talk to us, but we can usually see them, which sometimes presents some comical relief to what is transpiring.

Some of the sessions that we experienced were difficult to deal with as many times I physically went through a lot of pain; however, the pain left my body after the session. Denise felt much of the feelings that were occurring in my body and sometimes I felt them as they occurred in hers. We experienced these events whenever we were together, and many times during the night the Angels just jumped in unexpectedly. What an occurrence!

PROLOGUE

Nothing in my entire life prepared me for what I am now going to present to you as the story of my coming of age. I have decided to present this in chronological order and, as I stated in the Introduction, in two separate parts.

In the past year my life has taken a complete turn from where I had been. I have come to see and understand that in this life we are here to experience both down times and up times. Some of us choose to make the down times a little longer than others. I was one of those people.

To begin with, I never had a Near Death Experience, I never spoke to Angels or Spirit Guides, and I always had my feet firmly attached to the ground. I have recently become aware of the fact that this is not what our lives are all about. We are here because we chose to be here, and our Angels and Spirit Guides give us great Kudos for coming to this Earth to live for a short while on the Physical Plane. Angels have never been in physical form, which makes for some wry jokes at times. We chose to become flesh and blood and that choice we made before we came to Earth. We are highly respected for making this choice. Not everyone chooses to come into the physical and that is fine too. It's almost like someone choosing to become a teacher or a firefighter. It's just a choice.

There are no coincidences in this life. Since we have chosen to be here and are working our way back to our Godselves, many different avenues and choices are always presented. Everything we are doing now we have decided to do long before we came into this world. From the smallest baby passing on at birth, to the oldest living person, we have all chosen to be where we are. We have much to learn and that is why we keep coming back to Earth -- to learn more. Besides it being fun to be in the physical (because the physical is a very powerful draw on all spirits), we can learn so much from each other. Every day is a brand new learning experience for us. Some of my friends and family think that I am nuts, but I have found that everyone marches to the beat of his or her own drummer. And, I for one like the drumbeat that I am now hearing.

When I was a small child I remember the following, which has always stayed with me and never changed. I was about five or six-years old, and I remember playing in the yard at my grandparent's house. It wasn't a huge yard but at the time it was big to me. My sisters were there as well as an uncle of mine who is also my age. While we were playing I remember that all of a sudden we all were able to fly like Superman, within the confines of the backyard. This image is very vivid in my mind and has never changed from the perspective of adulthood, except for the fact that I no longer see it as possible. Also in the yard was a large bulldozer that was going to be used to repave the driveway at the time. I can see all of us getting on the pay loader, jumping off, and flying around the yard as if it was the most natural thing in the world

PROLOGUE

to do! I of course had the red Superman cape, which my sisters wanted from me, but I would not let them have it. But, I remember them being able to fly just like me even without a cape. We all had a ball that entire afternoon, and I remember some adult, I believe it was my grandfather, just walking by and not thinking anything of our type of playing in that yard. Maybe it was all a dream; yet, whether it was or not, I experienced it. This was the only time of my earlier life that something out of the ordinary happened to me, if it did.

Let's move on some thirty years or so to around 1990. It was around this time that I began to get the feeling that there was more to this life than I ever thought there was. I came across Bob Monroe's second book *Far Journeys*. At the time I did not know that this was his second book until I read it. I found his writings to be eye opening and interesting. Then I read his first book *Journeys Out of the Body* and was hooked. This began what turned out to be an almost fifteen-year quest to know as much as I could about the "other side". I began to read any metaphysical book I could find. It turned out that I must have been on the cusp of the trend happening at that time due to all of the books that were printed in the early 1990's about Out of Body Travel and Remote Viewing.

While delving into these new areas my personal life was changing, and I was unable to really do extensive training or research into these areas of the Astral Plane. So, I had to wait for a more opportune time. Actually, I had to wait until June of 2004 for my research to really take off. My children were grown and unfortunately I went through a divorce. Coincidentally, that is when my life went in a whole new direction. Anyone who has gone through divorce knows that the process takes a lot out of you emotionally and physically. Mine was no exception. However, you have to remember that everything happens at a specific time and for a specific reason. I was suddenly free to delve into Astral matters without interruption.

While going through my divorce and feeling really down at times, I decided to have a talk with God. I asked why this process was so hard, and why it took so long for things to get done. Well, I came to find out the reason. Many times I had heard the expression "God is my co-pilot"; therefore, I decided to tell God that He was going to drive my car, and He could just take me along for the ride. I figured that He should know where I am going. Immediately after I had done this, I noticed that a great weight was lifted off of my shoulders, I had a renewed outlook on everything, and things started to go my way for a change. This point was poignantly brought to my attention after many good things had begun to happen, and I just let things roll along. The very first thing I did after my divorce became final was to write a check to my lawyer and the next was to write a check to The Monroe Institute for a Gateway Voyage class. This is where everything began for me, and my life was profoundly changed forever.

Upon reflection about the timing of all of these matters, one thing stood out above all of the rest. That was the fact that, if things had not gone EXACTLY the way they did, I would not have encountered the many people that I now have as great friends and the many things that happened to me would have not come into play.

Part One

1

My First Visit to The Monroe Institute

The Monroe Institute (TMI) is an educational institution that explores profound states of expanded awareness that result in new approaches to ways of thinking and the experiences of being. Students often develop a different overview of their lives, and a changed perspective on their experiences. Life seems to take on a new significance.

The first class that everyone attends at TMI is the Gateway Voyage class. This is the class that introduces the Hemi-Sync methods and trains the student's mind how to expand beyond its normal realities. They use headphones and binaural beats to get the brain into hemispherical synchronization (Hemi-Sync). It is a patented method to expand awareness. You see, in this state the brain creates a third sound wave by listening to two different beats (one in each ear). This third-wave state enables the brain to enter into various and different expanded states of awareness, which are called Focus Levels. There are many Focus Levels that range from Focus 1 (which is our normal state of existence) up to approximately Focus 49. All of these Focus Levels occur on the Astral Plane.

TALKING WITH ANGELS

During the Gateway Voyage class you experience each of the Focus Levels up to Focus Level 21, which is called the "Café". The Café is actually a meeting place on Focus Level 21 where people can meet in the Ether and go exploring together into higher Focus Levels.

I took this first class in September 2004. TMI is located in the Shenandoah Valley in Virginia, and September is a wonderful month to be there. It was a seven-hour drive from my home in New Jersey to TMI, and I had the feeling that I was coming home, although I had never been there. This occurs every time I make the trip to TMI. I just love the surroundings and peacefulness of the mountains. Using their directions, I was able to find the complex easily. When I entered the grounds for the first time, I was bursting with the excitement that I would be learning how to do all of the things that I had only read about. I had to stop the car for a moment, give thanks to the Almighty that I had finally made it here, and drink in the beautiful and fresh mountain air. To me, it was heaven on Earth. It turned out to be more than I had even dreamed possible!

When I entered the Nancy Penn Center (where the class was to take place) for the first time I felt exhilarated and blessed that I was finally there. I checked in with a woman named Franceen who turned out to be the instructor for the class. She explained how everything worked at TMI. However, she did not tell me that they take your watch from you so time becomes irrelevant for the week. By taking everyone's watch from him or her on the first night of the seminar you become very free and put the outside world on the back burner for your entire stay there. With everyone arriving on the first day, you have time to look around and soak in the majesty of the mountains. You feel like you are in suspended time and experience the feeling that no one can touch the magic of the place. One of the most intriguing items on the grounds is the seven-foot high crystal that is on an open area behind the Nancy Penn Center. You see it and are immediately drawn to it. I am told that there is a very similar crystal at Roberts Mountain Retreat, which is the other center they have for classes and is about two miles further down the road. Just approaching the crystal you are in a state of awe at its majesty, and when you touch it for the first time, you usually have to pull back your hands because the feeling is not what you would expect. The crystal is alive and vibrating and the vibrations are so powerful they go right through you. At TMI you find out that you have to push aside all of your preconceived ideas that you had about life and reality. After a short while, everything makes much more sense to you.

Putting my suitcase and clothes away I was introduced for the first time to the "Controlled Holistic Environmental Center" (CHEC) units for sleeping and for listening to the Hemi-Sync tapes that were our training tools for the week. These CHEC units were two to a room and had a three-foot by three-foot opening to crawl into them with a heavy black curtain over the door to give you darkness during the exercises. There were headphones, a pillow with blankets, and three adjustable lights-- red, yellow and blue-- to adjust anyway you felt comfortable to produce a calming affect on yourself while listening to the tapes. My roommate was a sixty-five year old gentleman who was beginning his exploration to find out more about his nonphysical body. He was a true skeptic, and he was also an atheist. By the end of the week, he would be a changed person. He was a short, svelte man with long gray hair, a mustache and a beard that was mostly gray. He also wore glasses. After we made our introductions, it turned out that he was in the food catering business in Atlanta, Georgia. I told him that I was a firefighter from New Jersey and that I was very excited about the week ahead of us. He too was excited but his skepticism was already beginning to show through. He said that he had listened to all of the tapes at home and all he succeeded in doing was to fall asleep during each and every session. I told him that I had a similar problem myself and that I was hoping that by being here with all of the extra energy and surroundings I would be able to achieve something more. As it turned out, the energy and peacefulness and the beautiful participants in our class, made the entire week one of joy and happiness (to be drawn upon for a long time to come) and affected us both.

People were arriving all Saturday afternoon and I met a person who had a great familiarity to me. When I looked at him I said, "I know you" and his response was, "Of course you know me, we've shared many lives together". Now, this I was not used to. I have had those Déjà Vu experiences in the past as most of us have, but to find someone who just nonchalantly said that we had spent many lives together just blew me away. As the week unfolded he and I became great friends. At TMI it is not unusual for this type of thing to happen. You see, there are no coincidences in this life. Everything we do we have planned before we came into this physical dimension. All we have to do is to "remember" our past. I know this is much easier said than done, but it is achievable in this lifetime. Since this time, Thomas and I have become great friends as often happens in this part of Virginia.

It turned out that Thomas was attending this workshop with nine other people from their company, the Lightsource Group. Lightsource, at the time, was a new program that had married the Hemi-Sync sounds to a computer program that was designed to utilize any of the Sacred Geometric shapes that have come down through the centuries. These shapes run on the computer and you can run the Hemi-Sync along with them to give you an expanded awareness of your surroundings. There are two tracks on this program that can be repeated or you can add your own tracks to the volume. The Sacred Geometric shapes are designed to change with different colors going through all of the shapes, or you can lock-in whatever shapes or colors you prefer. This is a terrific program and one that everyone can enjoy for either entertainment or meditative purposes. All of the people from the Lightsource group were terrific people. Many of them live in Hawaii and traveled from there to be at this seminar. I was truly blessed to have been with these people.

The Gateway experience was one that people remember for the rest of their lives. It was truly a transformational event. I had never before had any paranormal experiences and I was never one to make up events in my mind. Gateway started out in the present and as the week progressed you were taken from Focus 1 through Focus 21. Along the way you experienced different levels of consciousness. During one of the sessions you are told to look for your guides. These are spirits who help you along the way as you explore what is beyond the veil. If you get stuck on a problem or have a question, your guides will be there to help you. Sometimes you have to ask them and other times they will just tell you what to do before you even ask the question.

I remember that I was walking along a stream when I saw an old black man standing in full farmer coveralls and a long sleeve shirt with the sleeves rolled up. When I saw him I did not know who he was. He said," You can call me Uncle Remus. I'm your guide." I thought that was quite funny and told him so. He said," Well, funny or not, that's the way it is." Since that first meeting I have not seen him in person again. However, he is always around and helps me a great deal but always from the vantage point of just showing up in my thoughts, not in bodily form.

2

First Past Life

My first past life regression was done several years ago with a woman whose name now escapes me. It was my first experience with past lives and with hypnosis. I have always felt an attachment to two specific periods in history. One of them was ancient Egypt, although not to any particular era or location. The other was a definite feeling that I had been in Napoleon's Grand Army and had been with him during the unsuccessful Russian Campaign where most of his troops succumbed to starvation and death after being lured deep into Russia during the late fall and early winter. That campaign would ultimately lead to his eventual downfall. When I was placed into a state of hypnosis for the first time I was unaware of what to expect. I had thought that I would go into a deep trance and that I would not remember what had happened during the session. I was pleasantly surprised to feel like I just had my eyes closed and was directed along a path to a cabin in the woods from which I would make my journeys. This cabin was lovely and of my own making. There was a fireplace and a rocking chair nearby with a blanket next to it in case I got cold; since it was wintertime when this was done.

TALKING WITH ANGELS

I was directed to go to a place that I needed to be, I immediately went to a dry sandy desert place where there were many people rummaging around and bumping into one another. As I began to get my bearings at this location, I realized that this was a typical bazaar that you would find in a nomadic area of the world. Looking at my dress I saw that I had sandals on my feet and a long whitish robe that would be typical for this climate. I had a long grayish beard, and I had something over my shoulder although I could not make out what it was. I walked along the street until I was out of the crowded area and on a side street. I approached a two-story dwelling, and I looked up to inspect it to be sure everything was in proper order. I got the impression that this was a daily routine for me to do this as I approached my home. I opened the door to a sandstone dwelling that was quite large on the interior, or at least felt large from my perspective. It seemed that I was a scribe in this lifetime, someone who was up a few rungs on the ladder, as I also had a set of stairs leading to the second floor where my bedroom was. I saw children running around and a woman with a teenage girl nearby assisting her with some type of detail, whether it was cooking or sewing I do not remember. However, they animatedly greeted me when I came in and rushed over to attend to my needs, whatever they might have been. It seems that in this time period (which I felt was around 42 B.C.) the women of the house would tend to the husband's needs before anything else was done. They took off my tunic and gave me a plain white gown to put on. They assisted me with this and gave me a cool drink afterwards. It seemed that the assistant to my wife was a slave girl that we had been given as a gift for doing some good deed for the ruler of the area. Looking around the one large room in the house, I saw sandstone walls with a few decorations on them. There was a large woven rug in the middle of the floor and a table with several chairs along one wall but few places for anyone to sit, except for some small cushions scattered about with short tassels on their sides. All of them seemed very worn and not very comfortable to sit on. A young girl came into the room and gave me a hug and a kiss; she had been my daughter in that life, and I got the impression that she was my daughter in this life also.

When I moved from that past life into the next one, the first thing that happened was that my body began shaking. I seemed to be freezing to death, and I needed a blanket to be placed over me so that I would not freeze. I realized that I was in a very cold place. As I looked around, all I could see was a frozen wasteland with few trees and a few houses which all looked abandoned. There were many dead bodies lying around, and horses with wagons attached were moving along a road very slowly and with much pain. Many of the men were wearing soldier's uniforms that were tattered and many had their feet tied up in rags. They no longer had boots on. I realized that I was in Russia with Napoleon's army during the fiasco where he had lost over seventy-five percent of his men, not due to battle but due to the cold conditions there. A very clever adversary had lured him into Russia; one who knew that the deeper his army got into Russia the more men would be lost. I knew that the French Army was eventually forced to retreat and during that retreat more than 200,000 troops were lost due to freezing and starvation. Napoleon's Army would never recover from this devastating loss. But my life went on for many years. It seemed that I had married and had a daughter who eventually grew up to be a famous singer on stage in Europe and married a man from the upper echelons of society. This girl was once again the same daughter that I have today.

3

Akashic Records

The Akashic is a theosophical term that refers to a universal database and universal filing system that records every thought, word and action of each individual everywhere that has ever lived. The location of the Akashic records is the Library in the Ether. The Library is a very real place. People's thoughts over the millennium have created it out of their thoughts, and have turned it into an actual physical place. The Library is much more than the Library of Alexandria.

It has been said that the Akashic records are similar to a Cosmic or collective consciousness. This collection of records has been referred to by many different names including the Cosmic Mind, the Universal Mind, the collective unconscious, or the collective subconscious. There are those who think that the Akashic records make clairvoyance and psychic perception possible.

It is also maintained by some that the events recorded upon the Akasha can be ascertained or read in certain states of consciousness using techniques that can be learned at The Monroe Institute. Thus ordinary people can and do perceive the Akashic records. Many mystics and yogis believe that these records can also be perceived in psychic states.

Some people in subconscious states are able to read the Akashic records. An explanation for this phenomenon is that the Akashic records are the macrocosm of the individual subconscious mind. Both function similarly and they possess thoughts, which are never forgotten. The collective subconscious gathers all thoughts from each subconscious mind, which can be read by some other subconscious minds. Marcel Proust said," The real voyage of discovery consists not in seeing new lands, but seeing with new eyes". This is how you can perceive in the Ether, with new eyes that allow you to see through the veil. This way you can explore areas of reality beyond the Physical Plane.

An example of a person many claimed to be able to read the Akashic records is the late American mystic Edgar Cayce. Cayce did his readings in a sleep state or trance. Dr. Wesley H. Ketchum, who for several years used Cayce as an adjunct to his medical practice, said that Cayce's subconscious was in direct communication with all other subconscious minds and was capable of interpreting through his own objective mind the impressions he received. Thus, Cayce was interpreting the collective subconscious mind long before the psychiatrist C.J. Jung postulated his concept of the collective unconscious.

4

After Gateway

(10/29/2004)

I met some exceptional people at TMI. Besides Thomas, I became friends with Jerry, Angel, Alan and Noriko. I shall be forever
grateful for our many talks. Thomas and I made a real connection
at TMI. He nonchalantly brushed it off as "Heh man, we were
meant to be here at this time, and we have spent many other lives
together before this!" Now this may be "normal" for Thomas,
but this is not normal for me. Although I now know we are more
than our physical bodies and that I have lived before, I had never
met anyone with whom I had contact with in any previous lives.
And, we have been on a trip ever since!

Before TMI, I told Thomas that if he was in New York City
for any shows in the future that he should give me a call. Well,
low and behold, there was a show there in mid-October, and
Thomas called me and asked if I wanted to give him a hand at
his booth selling Lightsource. I said, " No problem." But, I then
explained that I could only make two out of three days due to my
Fire Department job. His turn to say, "No problem", so I spent
two days at the show with him, and we had a fabulous time. We

met so many terrific individuals with such great energy that I was totally exhausted at the end of the weekend due to dealing with all of these people with such high energy levels.

When the weekend was over, Thomas and I spent some time together, and we really got to know each other. We found out that we both liked good Italian food for starters. Thomas was going down to his boat for a few days before his next show and invited me along, but I had to decline due to work obligations. Then he asked me if I wanted to go to the Philadelphia show the following weekend, but again I told him I had to work. However, God had other plans for me. On that Tuesday while at work I was moving a very heavy object when a pipe came out of nowhere and hit me on the head. I was not knocked out, but I did have an inch and a quarter gash in my head. I was taken to the emergency room at the local hospital and they stapled it shut with five staples. That was the first time I was actually stapled instead of sutured up for a cut. It was definitely different. But, this also gave me a week off from firefighting because the staples prevented me from wearing a fire helmet, so I had free time. Guess what I did? Right, I called Thomas who was down on his boat and told him that I was going to be able to make it to Philadelphia for the weekend.

The show was actually in Valley Forge right outside of Philadelphia. And what a great time we had again. From there we returned to my place in New Jersey because Thomas had to do a show with Jodi Serota on the following Wednesday in New York City at a local church. I think Thomas liked my place or maybe it was my high speed Internet that he was so surprised to find, since he cannot get high speed in too many places when he travels.

AFTER GATEWAY

I want to thank Lumin for making the first Lightsource program with the sound track of Enos Dream. For those who are not familiar with this Lightsource version, I would advise you to look into it. It is well worth your while. Lumin did this track with bioengineering, and it is designed to open your heart up for Love and Forgiveness. I personally had a tremendous spiritual experience while listening to this audio track, and for that I am truly grateful to Lumin and to all those who had a hand in making it.

When I returned from TMI last month, I called my daughter who was at college and told her about the exciting time that I had. After hearing me expound on the great things that had occurred, she said that she would like to go. She is very open minded about these things. I told her that I would like to send her and her brother, who is not open minded. He is an Astronautical Engineer and has his feet planted firmly on the terra firma of this good Earth. However, so far neither of them have attended, but I am hopeful that they will one day. When the time is right they will be drawn there.

The guys at my firehouse could not understand when I told them that they were not really looking at me, but they were looking at my feet because I was really standing ten feet off of the ground! I knew that I was smiling all day and night. I explained to them that TMI does definitely have a positive effect on your life. When I came back from the Gateway Voyage program they looked at me weirdly. I told them that if they think I was weird last time that they had not seen anything yet. However, I have to say that Franceen was right when she told me about people wanting to be around me after attending TMI. It's because we exude such tremendous energy, and they all feel better just standing close to us.

I put the Lightsource program on the firehouse computer and the guys ran it all day, with the Higher and Remembrance music along with the colors. They really liked the colors; it went along with the spinning disco ball of colors that they liked to turn on in the dormitory. It made our boss, the Deputy Chief, nuts when he saw it, but since he's a good guy, he walked away shaking his head. We have to have some fun at the firehouse since we live there for twenty-four hours at a time.

I received a terrific surprise when I came home on Friday. I was exhausted from the entire week, and I was taking a nap when my doorbell rang. It was my daughter! She came home from college for the weekend and dropped by to see me. She wanted to hear what I had experienced at TMI. I was ecstatic that she dropped by because I was bursting with all of the emotions from the week, and I just needed to tell someone. She was the perfect one to tell. There are no coincidences. She was very excited about all of it, and she said that she cannot wait to go there herself. God I love her so much. She is a terrific young person.

In my church they do Spiritual Healing at the start of services. I specifically went to a good friend of mine to see if he noticed a difference in me during the healing. He sure did! He said that there a was a beam of light coming from above directly into the center of my head, and he could not get any further down than my chest area above my Heart chakra. He said that the intense vibrations that he was feeling from the sides of my head made his hands shake, they were so powerful. He was really stunned at the energy that I was giving off. I could feel it too. I hoped that it did not go away too soon as I was enjoying it. When it did subside, I knew that I was still living in a higher plane of existence than I had been before.

5

Remote Viewing Class

My second class at TMI was the Remote Viewing (RV) class. Remote Viewing is a process that involves getting into a state of mind that allows you to access another time or place without leaving the room where you are. One perceives what is going on in any particular location that you are trying to view. The person, who teaches the RV class, Skip, is one of the people who ran the Remote Viewing project for the U.S. military. TMI also has the great privilege of having Joe McMoneagle, one of the best Remote Viewers on the planet, living right on their grounds.

One of the things that they do in this class is to ask you to draw the first thing that comes to your mind after an introduction of what RV is all about. They usually pick a target that has many unique properties that stand out visually. Many in the class were able to perceive some parts of the target right off the bat. Believe it or not, many people do very well in the beginning, because the conscious mind does not know what is going on yet. Once the conscious mind figures out that something is going on, it jumps right in with its' own perceptions of what should be, and everyone's percentage of correct answers drops dramatically. Skip said that that is not unusual for any class.

I found that RV can be done by just about anyone given enough time and practice. We only touched on the fundamentals of Remote Viewing, but there was enough information and training to prove that Remote Viewing does work. Even some of the skeptical people in the class came away with the conclusion that there was something to this. For my part I came away from this class with a much greater appreciation of what kinds of things the mind is capable of doing. I believe that this class was fundamental for my future travels due to the fact that with Remote Viewing you can perceive different times and different places at will.

6

Taking Off for the First Time

Today, I had my first experience with retrievals! I used the tape series "Going Home" from TMI. The tapes "Moment of Revelation" and "Touring the Interstate" were the two tapes that enabled me to go into these expanded awareness states, which I had been unable to perceive up to this point.

AND, WHAT A RIDE!!

The tapes took me to the Café in Focus 21. Focus 21 is the last altered state in the physical realm, and from Focus 22 on you enter the Astral Plane of existence. Focus 23 is the first level after the consciousness or soul leaves the physical body. Focus 22 is the level you enter when in a coma or other unconscious state prior to the physical death of the body. Focus 23 is the first state that you enter after you leave your body. Most people will pass through this level with no problem, but others (who may not have any idea of what happens after physical death, or who may not realize they have passed from the physical due to a sudden death) get stuck on this level and need someone to come along and help them move on. In Focus 23 we can help others to move on by taking them to Focus 27 where the Park is found.

The Park is an area you usually enter after death where you can meet friends and family that have previously passed on. You can also find the Center in the Park where you go to figure out what you want to do next.

In Focus 23 Bob Monroe (on the tape) told me to look around to see if I knew anyone there. As I was looking around, I saw a woman wearing a pink blouse and black slacks. She was about 60-years old, had grey hair, and was holding onto a shopping cart in a supermarket. I went over to her and asked, "Can I help you?

She told me that she would like to find her way out. Apparently, she had been there for a while and could not find the exit.

I asked her what was the last thing that she remembered, and she told me that she remembered just falling to the floor, and then there were a lot of people around helping her. I explained to her as delicately as I could that she had passed on from the physical body to a new realm. She took this rather well I thought. Maybe she had the thought herself while she had been waiting in the store. She looked thoughtful for a while and then she said, " What happens now? " I explained to her that if she wanted to leave the supermarket, I would be glad to help her find some friends that I knew would be waiting for her in the Park in Focus 27. She said, "That would be fine." I grasped her hand and we left the store through the ceiling and went on to Focus 27 where there were people waiting as I had told her. She thanked me for my help and just moved right into the group who had come to welcome her to her new existence.

TAKING OFF FOR THE FIRST TIME

This was my first experience with soul retrievals, and I did not think to ask for any verifying details of who she was or where she was from. What an exciting and unexpected journey it was. I thank Bob for the opportunity to have helped someone along the path from here to the next existence that awaits us all.

After I had helped this woman move on, I drifted back to Focus 23 for some reason, and what do you think I found this time?! Well, believe it or not, I found a fully decked out African hunter or medicine man in full Regalia. The first thing I thought was, "Oh my God, how do I talk to him?" A thought popped right into my head, obviously from my Spirit Guide, that I should "just talk to him". So I did! Believe it or not I was able to communicate with no problem. Now, I may have "Clicked out" because the only thing I can remember was that I took his hand, and he came with me through Focus 24, but somewhere between Focus 25 and Focus 26 he just disappeared from my site like a wisp of air, or a ghost if you like. The only thing that I can think of is that I know that the levels between Focus 24 to Focus 26 are different religious levels, and I can only think that he was pulled towards an area that was to his liking and he just went....Poof! At least I moved him on from Focus 23.

This was just an incredible experience for me. I hope each of you have similar journeys of your own. I found out the last time that I was at TMI that the Going Home series was never a big seller. I guess no one wants to stare down their own mortality directly in the face. Recently people have found out that you can get from Focus 22 to Focus 27 by using these tapes. I for one can attest to the fact that they *do* work.

I told my daughter about these experiences, and she was excited about the whole thing. She asked me questions about the Focus levels and where the people go if they disappear while you are taking them to a new level. Also, she wanted to know how you find these people. It was just so exciting to have her to talk to about these things and see her anticipation of experiencing these things for herself. I felt like a Blessed individual.

The same day while listening to either "Right of Passage' or "Homecoming" (they are all A and B sides in the "Going Home" series) I found that I was in Focus 27 at the Park. I came across a friend from the Fire Department who entered the job with me, but was killed in a motorcycle accident a year ago. He said, "Hi Mate" which was his usual greeting. I told him that I had looked for him once or twice before, but I could not find him in the Ether. He said that he knew that I was looking for him, but he had been busy those other times. But this time he made it a point to come to me. I told him that he still owed me a day of work, because I had worked for him a day during the summer of the year he died. He had planned to pay me back at Christmas, but he died that fall. He just laughed and said, "Sorry 'bout that Mate". I told him that it had been my pleasure to allow him to spend an additional day with his family before passing on. He appreciated that too. We said our good-byes, and we went our separate ways.

Then someone else came into view at the park. This person was my sister-in-law who had passed a few years ago from breast cancer at the age of 32. She had three little girls all under five years old at the time. She looked like the beautiful person that she was before the cancer with beautiful full flowing hair and a bright infectious smile. She had always been a person to light up any room that she entered. We spoke for a few minutes, and she knew all about what was happening on the physical plane. I guess a mother's love never dims. She said she was happy that her husband had found someone else who took the three girls and him in, which is not very often these days. She said that she was very busy where she was now. I told her that she looked ravishing, and she thanked me and said that we would meet again sometime. So she moved on, and I was left sitting on the bench by myself with my thoughts about what had just happened. Now, I know that these things did happen, but I do not have any proof that would be useable but that is okay with me. I was not on this journey for anyone else, only myself.

7

Transmuting Thoughts
to God

Thomas told me about transmuting our thoughts directly to God. This is a very powerful tool to have in your toolbox. When Thomas and I spoke about it, he told me that was the way he deals with any problem that confronts him that he cannot seem to deal with. However, even though I understood the concept of transmuting thoughts directly to God, I did not understand how it really worked. It is much like learning anything new, it takes time. I just kept reading his Sacred Geometry interview on his website over and over again. I concentrated on the parts that were about the transmuting of thoughts to the Light. After about two months of working on this, I have finally been able to do it! WHAT A POWERFUL TOOL IT IS!!

You don't have to ask God for anything. You send out the thoughts about the problem directly to God and very quickly after that you get a feeling of calmness that comes over you and the problem that you were concerned with is no longer of concern to you! The resolution of the matter seems to take care of itself. Now, I know this sounds off the wall, but I can only relate to you my own experiences and try to put them into words. I am coming to find that words are a very poor way to try to explain thoughts, actions and happenings that are going on inside your mind. But, words are the only tools that we have to try to communicate with to one another in this physical realm.

I went from a person who believes in many things to a person who knows that the things I have set forth in this book are real. And I encourage each and every one of you to experience these things for yourselves so that you too can gain a better understanding of this life in the physical that we are all dealing with right now.

I took my children to see "What the Bleep". They both liked it very much. Of course, the analytical mind of my son had many questions, so I referred him to their website to get some books that could provide him with some answers, and then I emailed him the TMI website and told him to look under the research portion of the site for articles which would give him some scientific background on the whole Hemi-Sync process, to try to get him to be a little open minded about TMI for himself. You can lead a horse to water... but I do have hopes for him.

8

The Center

I just took my first visit to the Center; this certainly is where the action is. The Center is the place where we all go to figure out what we want to do next Actually, it is a way-station place where people can also get medical assistance if they passed on from a physical ailment, or any other treatment or type of aid that they may need. I started out in Focus 27 with my usual walk along the stream by way of a slowly winding path that has pansies running along the side. I always liked pansies for some reason. I guess maybe it's because they look like they are smiling all the time. On the left side of the path was this huge weeping willow tree, another of my favorites, with a couple sitting having a picnic beneath it. There was a bright beautiful and sunny blue sky with a few bellowing cumulus and nimbus clouds overhead. It was just so beautiful a place to be that sometimes I feel like staying and never coming back, but I really had so much I wanted to do. I walked up past the pond where people were sitting on the redbrick wall that surrounded it.

There were a great many people speaking various languages all around me and for some reason I could understand each of their conversations. The Center has fifty-foot tall towering spires on the two front edifices and a large center door made of glass that is at least thirty-feet tall, with many designs on the glass doors for decoration. The doors open and close automatically as you approach. I climbed the few short stairs leading up to the huge doorway, turned around to view the Park, and I just could not believe that I was actually there. This was such an incredible moment that I had to stop, take a deep breath of clean fresh air, and just enjoy my being in such a place.

As I turned again to go through the door at the Center, I was overwhelmed by the momentous occasion that I was experiencing. I had been to the Park several times but not up to the Center. I still had the feeling that I was not supposed to go into the Center since I was still in the physical. However, now that I was there I figured that I might as well experience it. Therefore, I entered. But once I was inside, the Center revealed itself in its entire glorious splendor. There were huge beautiful chandeliers hanging imposingly from the ceiling in various places. I could see that the hallways, which spread out in many directions, go on for what seemed to be forever. The walls were covered with various murals and the sidewalls appeared to be going up and curving into partial dome shapes centering on the chandeliers in the center. The floors were made of beautiful white marble and were shimmering like a mirror. People were busy mulling about and taking care of their own business or helping others with theirs.

As I looked at the front wall area I was immediately struck by the fact that it was more like an airport than a way station. There were many little tables with two or three people sitting at them in very animated discussions. There was even a check-in area, like at an airport, but what it was for I didn't know. It seemed a little out of place, but I guess they have to take care of business at the Center too. Many people just want to move on to their next adventure; presumably they knew what they wanted even before they got here. I was wondering what state of mind I would be in when it is my turn to step up to the Center for my next adventure. Maybe I should take some time to think about it, so that I'll know what to do when I arrive there for real.

Before I entered the building I asked my guide to stay with me, as I would probably need him soon. As I was surveying the scene, a woman who was waving at me caught my attention. I wasn't sure that she was motioning to me at first, but when I asked her with a shrug of my shoulders if it was me she wanted, she acknowledged that it was I. I strolled over to her, and she introduced herself as Angela. She said that she would be my guide through the Center for this trip. I was surprised that she knew that I was coming, but then I thought about it for a second and realized that she knew that I would be here at this time, so it was not surprising to find someone there for me. Angela asked me where it was that I had wanted to investigate today. I told her that I really would like to see the Library, because from what I have learned, the Library is where the real action happens. She said, "That would be fine". We walked over to an elevator with bright shiny golden doors and brown marble running up the sides in very ornate designs and stepped in. She said that the Library was on the third floor.

This is where my first adventure into the Library unfortunately ended. I cannot remember any more from this journey. I must have clicked out. So, I will have to wait until I can re-enter the Center and continue my journey. Please understand that I am explaining these events to you as best I can as I remember them as they occurred to me. So, if some of these adventures are disjointed, that is the way they occurred.

9

Second Retrieval

This is SSOOOO CCOOOOLLLL...My second retrieval ! ! !

After going to Focus 27 and asking my guide if there was any-one to meet there, which there was not, I said, "Well, let's go to Focus 23 to see if there is someone at that level that I can help." So, that's where we went.

When I first arrived and started to look around, I didn't see anything. Then, all of a sudden I saw this pair of legs from the knee down. They were bare knees with white socks in saddle shoes. At first I didn't understand what I was looking at, since I just saw these legs, which were set on the sidewalk leaning over a short 18-inch fence. Then I saw a girl start to get up, and I could see that she had fallen or tripped over this short fence area and was just getting herself together. I went over to help her, and she thanked me for helping her up. She said that someone had pushed her and no one would help her get back up. That's when I knew what had happened to her. She was about twelve years old and had a Catholic School gray-plaid skirt and a maroon sweater vest on. I remembered to ask her name and where she was from. She said that her name was Patti Nimcus from Washburn, Illinois.

I asked her when she was born, and she said 1954. Now I had something to check, if I could remember it when I got back. So, I told my left-brain to remember this information for me.

I asked her, how long she had been there. She said it had been "awhile" but she just could not get herself up over the fence. I asked," What happened when you fell? She said that she remembered falling and hitting her head. I explained to her that when she hit her head, she had apparently hit it hard enough to cause her to die. She said, "No I didn't, I just fell". This was interesting work, when you had to convince someone that they were not in the physical world anymore. I asked her to pick up this piece of paper on this desk. Don't ask me how we got into a classroom but that is where we were. Of course, she could not pick up the piece of paper, and she slowly began to realize that I was telling her the truth about not being alive anymore. Patti said, "What happens now?" I asked her if she had any relatives that she had known that had passed on. She said her grandparents had passed on. I informed Patti that I could take her to them if she would like me to. She said, "That would be nice". I took her hand, and we took off towards the sky, but she did not quite understand what we were doing, and we shortly ended up at the Park. She loved the Park with the stream and the flowers. As we were walking along next to the stream, she noticed her grandparents up ahead and took off running to be with them with a great smile on her face. They hugged her and greeted her in the nicest way. As they were walking away, Patti turned around and gave me a big smile and yelled, "Thank You" as she walked off into the Center with her family members.

SECOND RETRIEVAL

I felt much satisfaction at having been able to help this little girl to move on to the next part of her journey.

Now, I had to check to see if any of the information that Patti had given me could be verified. I did a Google check and indeed I found that there is a town, Washburn, Illinois. It is tiny town of 1,100 people. I did a name check but did not come up with any family name Nimcus. Of course, I may be spelling it wrong and this girl had apparently died in the mid 1960's, so the family may no longer live there. There is a Catholic Church, but I do not know if there was a school there in the 1960's. If I really searched I guess I could find out more details of the town, but I am not going to do that. I am satisfied that there is at least a town of that name within the state.

Now, I went back to Focus 23 after this trip with Patti since I still had time. It was a bit far fetched (even for me), and I do not recall all of the details, as I must have clicked out for some part of this. What I found was a Knight in Armor. I know this is crazy and I thought, "You have got to be kidding me." I thought this out loud to my guide, and he just stood silently aside as usual. I am going to have to have a talk with my guide when I take the Guidelines class because he is not too much help to me most of the time, and I am quite frequently on my own with these things. But, I do have to admit that he does help me out when I am stuck, and I ask him for help. Although I just get his help as a thought in my mind rather than him communicating directly to me. However, I'll take his help any way he sends it to me, because when I ask for it, I am at a loss, and I do need his help.

Getting back to my Knight... as I said, I could not believe it was a real Knight, but it was! I had to ask him what in the world he was doing here, and he could not tell me. He did not remember what had happened to him except that it had something to do with his horse. It did not appear to be from a jousting event, but rather from some other event that had happened to him atop his mount. He did not remember a battle, so I was at a loss to explain to him what had happened. As I stated earlier, I am not quite sure what transpired here because I must have "clicked out" myself during some part of this. The next thing that I can recall is that he agreed to accompany me to Focus 27. I took his hand which had a metal glove over it, (a very strange feeling I might add), and we lifted up towards the sky. I asked his name, and he said Sir something, but I cannot remember what it was. I have to apologize for not giving too much detail here but I am telling you whatever I can remember. I must write as soon as possible after these trips so I don't forget the details. However, the next thing that I can recall is that we were at the Park and walking up to other Knights in Armor that he apparently knew because he seemed very happy to be with them. They quickly retreated to the Center and they disappeared before I could say anything more to the Knight.

I do have one more story to convey. The other day, it was only one retrieval after the Knight retrieval, I remember writing down a person's name and address, which is as follows: Tom Ripkin, 721 Hauser Lane, Columbia, South Carolina. I cannot remember where I found him or what time frame he was in or any other details, all I could remember was that I wanted his full address so that I could look it up when I got back. The only thing that

SECOND RETRIEVAL

I could verify was that Columbia is the State Capital of South Carolina. I did not find any Ripkin, but, then again, I did not know what time frame to look for.

✹

NOTE: I did the following retrieval this morning and decided to include it here because it is short. I had found this boy in an earlier retrieval, but I did not have the time to pursue him at that point. Therefore, I went to get him this morning. It appeared that he had been waiting a long time.

(1/17/2005)

John Limenkie, 11 years old, was playing baseball and was hit on the side of the head with the ball. He was wearing those old three-quarter pants that kids used to wear in the 1940-s. When I asked him when and where, he said it was 1943 in Spartensburg, Ohio. There is no Spartensburg, Ohio, but I may not have the spelling correct.

Anyway, he was sitting in a corner crying by himself, and I asked him, "Why are you crying?" He said, " The other kids would not play baseball with me anymore." He could not understand why. I explained to him that they couldn't play with him anymore because he is not there anymore. He did not understand what I was talking about, so I had to show him. I brought him over to the batters box and asked him to pick up the bat. When he could not do this, he said, "WOW!" But he still did not understand why. I tried to explain to him the best that I could about being dead, but he would not believe me.

I tried a new approach. I told him that I could take him where his friends were playing ball and that he would be allowed to play too. This got his attention. He said that all he wanted to do was to play ball. I said "take my hand and I will take you where your friends are playing ball right now." He jumped up and grabbed my hand. As we started to rise up he looked back at the ground and was a bit frightened. He said, "Am I going to be Okay?" I told him that everything was going to be fine. We reached the stream at the Park (this is my own preferred way of entering) and he began to feel more comfortable. As we started to walk along the stream, he saw a baseball game going on and took off for it. I yelled to him," Have a good time", and watched as his friends greeted him and welcomed him into the game.

10

The Library

This morning I decided to take a trip back to the Library. It seemed like "The place to be." I went back, and as I did not get too far the last time, I restarted at the front door of the Center. As I entered and started to look around, I spotted Angela waiting patiently for me. She said, "I'm here to help you today." So I said "Thank You". She asked if I still wanted to go to the Library, and I said that's exactly what I wanted to do. So we went over to the elevator and went down to the third floor. Don't ask me why we went down, but that is what the elevator said. As the door opened, we were outside (It seemed really strange, but considering where I was I guess it is not too strange). Angela pointed over to my right and said, "That is the Library". She said that I would meet someone inside the Library who would help me. She said, " Just go up the stairs and inside there would be a receptionist to help you with your needs."

Now, this is what I call a Library! The building was taller than the New York City Library, and it covered just about as much area, as far as I could tell. First of all, the front façade was gorgeous with huge Roman columns rising 70-80 feet in the air.

They were made of dark marble with gold leaf around the base of each. But the most impressive part of this façade was that you had to walk up at least thirty stairs to reach the entrance. It appeared to be a pretty far hike. As I started the upward climb, and being somewhat lazy myself, I said to myself that there had to be an easier way. Sure enough, my guide said, "Look, you are not in the physical, you can fly up to the top, if you'd like." I said, "You're right, what a great idea." But, I didn't actually fly; I just sort of skimmed over the top of the stairs with ease to the main entrance. The front façade also had a great many large windows through which you could see a beehive of activity going on. What a gorgeous site this Library was, it just blew me away. You could tell that this is the place to be, if you wanted to know any information.

I looked around from my vantage point on the top of the stairs and saw a beautiful valley below, not unlike the view at TMI. It was truly breathtaking. I took a long look, and then I stepped into the Library. What a place! There were crystal chandeliers hanging everywhere, the walls were made of wood paneling, there were marble floors down every hallway, and pictures were hanging on the walls of every size and description. There was a very enlightening atmosphere in the air. As I approached the main help desk, there was a person standing there busily taking care of some type of document. He slid down his glasses over his nose and asked me (not impolitely, but like a person who has been interrupted from a task they are trying to finish), if I needed help. I said, "Yes, this was my first visit to the Library so if someone could show me around that would be greatly appreciated."

THE LIBRARY

He sort of guffawed at what I said to him, and he said, "What do you mean this is your first visit, you come in here all the time to do research". This quite literally blew me away as I had no recollection of ever being here before. I remembered that in one of Bruce Moen's books he said something very similar about the Library when he first visited it. So, I said to him, "Well, this is my first conscious visit to the Library." I also said, "I am still in the physical right now and I don't have any control over what my soul does at night when I am sleeping." This made sense to him and he was a little bit more responsive.

He called over another person, Marty, to take care of me. I explained to Marty that this was my first visit, and I was just basically trying to find out the layout of what was where and what kind of things I might find. Marty seemed very pleased to have the opportunity to show someone around. I could tell he took much pride in the Library; it was like his own. We started from where we were standing, and Marty pointed out different areas. He said the front portion of where we were standing had a sitting room area where people could go to have conversations or just "read". However, reading there is not the same as reading here. They had viewing machines that helped you look for what you wanted. As we walked around, Marty was very animatedly explaining the different areas of knowledge to be found, and he pointed upstairs to the second floor which opened to the first, like a grand gallery, and said "back there" pointing upwards and towards the back of that room, "is our History Department" He explained that it was not a regular history department, but was one in which you could find out about unwritten history from the past. Now, that intrigued me to no end, since I have always wanted to know more about our lost history -- like the Pyramids (when and how were they built), and the Sphinx (who built it and when), etc.

Other areas included the Science Research Center, and I asked, "Don't you guys know everything up here?" Marty answered quite simply "No". I was surprised, but then again I guess I should not have been, since there is so much information to be known, that learning, even in the non-physical carries on and on. He showed me the research areas for science. These were glass-enclosed rooms with wood paneling only half way up the walls. The top half was all glass so you could see right into where the research was being done. It looked very interesting, and I made a note to myself that I would have to explore this area further when I had the time.

Next, we came to the best place of all. We turned a corner and there was a very long hallway that seemed to go on forever. Marty said, "This is the Past Lives Center." Now we were talking! Past lives was right up my alley as I wanted to know much more about myself and the different aspects of myself, and this seemed like the place to stop and do it. So, I said to Marty, "Can I stay here?" He said, "Sure, you can stay anywhere you want to." I asked him how it all worked and I was shown a machine that looked up your past lives. Since there are many past lives for many people, they are separated out by centuries and millennium. I asked to look at my file, and we went over to the machine and put my name in. Low and behold we found that I had been around the block many times before. They had records of me from several thousand years ago. This was pretty cool if you think about it. It was almost like finding the Great Library at Alexandria and finding that you had been there too. Something drew me to one section that was simply stated as "The 1400's". So, we took this file out. Marty explained that to view this information you had to use the machines that were set up by the desks. We found an empty one, and he explained the operation of the machine. Simply stated, the machine was a movie of your past lives. But, as you viewed it, you not only viewed as a person watching a movie, you became the participant with yourself from that bygone era of time. I said, " You have got to be kidding me!" Marty looked at me with a dumbfounded look, as if I had just challenged him to a duel at 20 paces. He said," That is the way it works, you participate in your own past lives that are being seen on the projector." I said, "I have got to try this!" Marty showed me how to set up the machine and how to operate the controls. He said it takes some getting used to since you become a participant and the projectionist, you sometimes get confused with the controls and some people have gotten "lost" inside the movie. I didn't quite understand that, but I said, "Let's give it a try." I sat down and turned this viewing machine on. The first thing that I saw was a jungle that looked very hot and wet. I started scanning and I began to get images in my mind (pretty good, since this whole trip was in my mind), and I was now watching something that was happening in my mind. It is just too complicated for me to try to understand. I just accepted that it was happening to me. I became this South American Indian fellow with very dark skin, and a broad flat nose and big feet, which seemed far too big for the body I was in. There was another person with me, who apparently was a friend. He was somewhat shorter than I was, and he had a very playful look and feel about himself. I knew this person, but I could not figure out who it was at the time. We were going through this jungle looking for some game to eat, and I kept slipping on the rocks that we were climbing over because they were all wet from the conditions around us. My companion seemed to get a big charge out of me falling all the time, as he seldom fell. This seemed to be the point where I had to go, or I clicked out, because I only remember being back at the Library telling Marty "Thank you, for the visit" and returning to the here and now. Later, the more I thought about it, I think my friend in the jungle was Thomas, but I cannot verify that. However, I wouldn't be surprised, as he had stated that he and I had traveled many roads together.

11

Is this Confirmation that it is All Real?

I was wondering if this was all real. The following story is from another adventurer out there that I send my adventures to. She is a woman from my church who had been taking trips into the Ether all of her life. She has never had any contact with TMI. Her story was really interesting to me. It showed me that there is definitely something going on, even if we did not consciously remember all of it. She told me that she would not tell me of our adventure together because if I did not remember it on my own, then I was not supposed to know of this adventure at this time. I am content with that, as I feel that we will know things when we are supposed to know them.

This occurred at the Library when she was out on her own adventure. Even she was surprised by the whole episode, which she set forth as follows:

You know it is real, so don't doubt yourself.... I wish I could tell you, but you know that even if I did, it probably wouldn't make any sense because you wouldn't remember where I took you. I truly believe that you will remember, when you are supposed to I'm not trying to seem arrogant in any way, and I hope that I'm not coming off like that. I don't want you to think that that's why I won't tell you, because its not. I really thought you knew, or would remember the trip, and that was why I asked you. I even don't remember how it ended, I don't remember bringing you back to the Library, or my last words to you.

Like I said, it happened really freakily, to me, one minute I was talking with my Angels, and the next minute I was with you in the Library, asking you if you wanted to go somewhere with me. This has never happened before like this, so, it obviously happened for a reason. What that reason was, your guess is as good as mine right at this moment, but if I get anything, I will definitely let you know, okay? . If I get any guidance on the matter, and I'm told that it's okay to discuss it with you, then I will. But nothing has been said, so I'm at a loss here, and I don't want to do anything that might screw something up, you know? I'm far from perfect, and from knowing it all.

12

Standstill

(1/22/2005)

I am presently at a standstill. I don't know why, but I have not been able to focus on anything in Focus 23 or Focus 27. I can look around in Focus 23 but it does not seem that there is anyone around that needs my help. I go to Focus 27 and get to the Library and search my past lives file, but I cannot seem to get into any of the things that I have done. I had been looking at my file for 2500 B.C., when the pyramids were built, but I could not obtain any information either on how the pyramids were built, or on what my life and what my participation was at that time.

I went back two times to try to address this, and I have come up empty both times. I cannot understand why I am being blocked. Maybe there is information that I am not supposed to know right now about that time period.

I just had a thought as I am writing this. If I am not supposed to know this information right now, maybe I should try something else in the Library, either a different time period, or a totally different area of exploration. I had not done a complete overview of the Library since I had been there. I got so interested in exploring my own past life that I did not go any further to see what else is there. I think the next trip back I will ask Marty to show me other areas to explore as I am sure there are many that I would be interested in.

(1/24/2005)

I did go back to Focus 23. I found a large black Indian type of woman who had been sacrificed by drowning. This had to have been a long time ago as she was wearing attire that would only be found in the jungle of some long forgotten tribe. I spoke to her; I still cannot believe that by speaking we all understand each other no matter what language is native to us. But, she seemed to understand why they sacrificed her; yet she was stuck in Focus 23. I felt that she was really close to where she was supposed to be, so I asked her if she wanted to come along with me to where she would find her friends. She calmly got up out of the water and came along with me. As soon as we hit Focus 25 she disappeared, which was what I had figured would happen to her, as she did not really feel that she was lost. Focus 24 and Focus 25 are spiritual realms where different religious beliefs can be explored. With that done, I continued on to Focus 27 and I sat on the wall by the pond for a while contemplating what I could do to remedy my situation. I finally figured that I should go back into the Center and try to figure out my problem. That's what I did. I found Angela, and explained my situation to her, but I must have clicked out at this point because I do not remember anything beyond that.

STANDSTILL

(1/25/2005)

I decided to go back to the Library and do some research on Unwritten History. I found Marty, and he took me up the black wrought-iron spiral staircase that leads up to the second level in the back to that area. I told him that I would like to find out more about the Sphinx in Egypt. He said, "Sure, no problem". We started to go through the files until we found one that simply said "Sphinx". He said, "Here you go", and he asked if I would need his help with the viewer. I told him I thought that I remembered how to use it. He said that he had other things to do but would be available if I needed him. I thanked him and found a viewer to go through the file. As I started to view the file, I was shown an area that was all covered with a glass dome. I did not understand where this could be, then I started to see people with these silver one-piece suits on that zipped up in the front, and I said to myself, this cannot be related to what I am looking for because it is too futuristic, and I am looking for something that happened twelve thousand years ago. But, as usual, it seems that what you expect to find, and what you do find, are two completely different things. I asked my guide for help, and was told that I was in the correct place. As I was looking around, all of a sudden I spotted the woman from my church who said that she met me at the Library the other day. I said, "What in the world are you doing here?" I asked her if this is where she took me the other day. I don't recall her answer.

The two of us started to look for someone to help us. Finally, we attracted the attention of someone, and they came over to us and asked what we needed. He introduced himself as "Skevin". I said, "We were looking for information on the Sphinx." He explained to us that the Sphinx was just constructed for "FUN". I said, "That cannot be true." He insisted that it was. I asked where we were, and he said, "This is Atlantis of course". That just blew me away! Although I had a feeling that that was where we might be, I just felt that it was inconceivable that I could actually be there. He assured us that we were actually in Atlantis, and he just walked away. So, we just looked around the place trying to get a feel for where we were and what timeframe we might be in. It did seem that we were in a very ancient time relative to today, but we could not put our finger on any exact timeframe. Ancient would not be too bold to say. My understanding is that Atlantis existed about 12,500 years ago, although this has not been confirmed by anyone.

(1/26/2005)

The Library seemed to be the place to explore for me right now, so I took another trip to see what I could find out. Upon entering I ran into Marty and told him that today I would like to look up Jesus Christ.

I started for the stairs to the Unwritten History gallery but Marty said that "No, the information I was looking for was in the Religion section of the Library." So we walked over to this area on the first floor, and Marty began sliding these huge walls that held files on them. Each wall opened up to a very long corridor, but to my surprise, he slid each wall one into the other, and they just flattened out so as to not take up any space. I know this is hard to conceptualize but these walls just folded right into each other as though they were no longer there. When you take your own trip to the Library you'll understand what I am talking about. Anyway, he finally stopped folding these walls together and said, "This is where we want to be." The hallway was extremely long, but we did not have to go far to find what we were looking for. Marty pulled out this one file, which simply said "Jesus Christ". He handed it to me and showed me over to a viewing machine. I thanked him for his help and sat down to view the file. The first thing that I became aware of was the time of year when Christ was born was in late February or March, cold but not the middle of winter either. I did not see who was there, but I did see the three Magi coming to where He was born to bring Him gifts. I moved on from there to when He was about ten-years old. I saw Him playing with two other boys, one whose name was Aaron and the other I did not get a name. But, I got the distinct impression that these two other boys were His brothers! Church teaching does not tell us that, but I had heard that He did have other siblings in the household. I was still looking at this file, when something told me to put it away as there was other information for me to ascertain. I placed this file back in the wall area and was drawn to the Past Lives area one more time where I had previously been.

I was drawn to a file of my past lives that simply said 2100 B.C. I pulled this file and began to go through it. I found this very old woman who had on a gray shoal that was wrapped over her head. She was in the local bazaar area where everything was sold, and she was making a rug made of straw or something similar. I got the impression that this was I. She was very old and had arthritis in her fingers, was hunched over, and very much into the work at hand. She would not be interrupted by anyone in the street or even anyone else within her own selling booth that was set up. She had her job to do and that's all she was concerned with. So, I took a little trip down the street to see what else was going on, and it was just a typical Mediterranean bazaar that one would even find today. As I was walking back towards this old woman again I could see what she was thinking. She was thinking about the time when she was seven or eight-years old, and she was playing in the river with some other friends. They were all having a great time splashing and having fun. Something told me that that was the only time in her life that she had ever been happy, and that everything since had been hard work with no relief. This was such an intense a feeling I had to go back and see if this was what I was actually feeling, or if I was mixing up two different events. No, I was not mixing two events together, and it just made me feel so sad that this woman only had that short period of time in her life that she was able to be a happy child or even an adult for that matter. I guess the times were hard and everyone just accepted life for what it was.

I could not stay there any longer due to the intensity of those feelings. I looked around to try to get a fix on a particular area or time frame, but I was unable to do so. With nothing else in this area calling out to me, I decided to leave because it was just too intense for me to stay there. I do not know why I was drawn there to begin with, or what else there was for me to find, but maybe it was just an experience in one of my past lives that was shown to me as part of the mosaic of who I am today.

13

Jerry

(1/29/2005)

I went on an adventure to try to find my friend Jerry from my TMI class since he had stated that he saw me at the Café. I told him that I had seen him there too and that we should go on a trip together. I went to the Café, and asked him if he wanted to join me for a trip to Focus 27. He said that he had not been there yet. We started in Focus 21. I told him we would go through Focus 22 to 27 and that he may get drawn to some other area along the way. As we passed through Focus 23 I asked him if he was drawn to anything here in particular. He said "No", so we continued on. As we approached Focus 26 we were suddenly at this stable of horses. I told Jerry, I guess we did have to make a stop in Focus 23, as I knew that's where we were right now. He took it in stride as I said that there must be someone here that we have to help. We came to a horse's stall with the number 11 on it. The horse was a beautiful medium -brown color (with a dark brown mane) with the nicest coat I had ever seen. We looked around to see if there was someone who needed help, but we could not find anyone. I asked my guide for help and was told to open the gate where the horse was, and we would find what we were looking for. I told Jerry that we were in the correct place and proceeded to open the gate. The horse was not quite sure what we were doing, but he moved aside for us to enter his stall. Upon entering we saw that there was an adolescent boy crouched down in the corner. We told him not to be afraid, as we were there to help him.

I said to Jerry, "This looks like one for you since you were a school teacher for so many years." He said, "Thanks a lot." He asked the boys' name. The boy said that his name was Toby, and he was waiting, but he did not seem to know what he was waiting for. Jerry asked, "How did you get here?" Toby said that he only remembered being sick. So Jerry asked him what sickness he had. He did not know, but he kept getting sicker. Jerry tried to explain to Toby that he was no longer in the physical world, but Toby did not believe him. We asked him if he remembered people not talking to him or ignoring him. He said, "Yes, that's why I'm in the stall because everyone ignored me." He felt more comfortable being by the horse because the horse acknowledged his presence. We tried to explain to him that the reason people ignored him was that he had passed from the physical, and they could no longer see him. Jerry asked him if he knew a priest, he said, "Yes", but then Jerry qualified it by saying, "A priest who had died." Toby said, "No". We then asked him if there was anyone that he knew who had died, and he said that there was an aunt of his that had died, but that he did not like her because she was very strict. We explained that we could take him to where she was, but he did not like that idea. I told him that she would no longer be very strict with him, and that she would be happy to see him. He warmed up to that idea since he had not been able to communicate with anyone else around the barn.

We took him by the hand and started off for Focus 27. As we approached Focus 27 Jerry was very excited since this would be his first trip there also. We approached the Park (as I usually do) from the stream leading up to the Center. Jerry remarked how beautiful it was, and Toby seemed to like it too. As we were walking along the path Jerry spotted some priests that he knew. I told him to go over and speak to them because I was sure they were there to meet him. I told him that I have met many people that I have known who had passed. As Jerry moved over to greet his friends, Toby saw his aunt up ahead waiting for him with a big smile on her face. I told him it's okay to go over to her. He said that he wasn't sure that he wanted to because she was so strict. I told him that everything would be fine, that she was here to greet him and to take him on to see other friends and family members. So Toby took off in her direction as he thanked me for my help. I said, "That is what I was here to do."

So now being by myself, I just decided to sit down on the wall and just enjoy the beautiful day. As I was sitting there enjoying the sunshine, someone called my name. It was an aunt of mine who had passed several years before. I walked over to her and asked, " How are you doing?" She said, "Fine." She explained that she had this important job now of directing people where to go for certain things. I said, "Yes, that is important because I am still lost when I come here and I have been here several times now." She said," It isn't really that hard once you get to know where everything is." I said," I'll keep trying." I told her that her husband, my uncle, is doing well and that his birthday just passed. She said that that was why she came there; I was to give him a message. I agreed to do this, but I added, "Will he believe me?" She said that he would because she was going to give me a word that he would recognize that was from her.

So I said, "What do you want me to tell him?" She said to tell him that she was doing fine, and that they would be together again when it was his time to cross over, and that she would be waiting for him when he arrives. I did not ask when that would be because we should not know these things. I asked her what the word was that he would recognize, and she said "beetlesburg or bartlesberg". I'm not sure I know which it was, but I know it's close. I told her that I would pass it on to him. (I have not seen him, but when I do, I will be sure to say that word to him and ask him if it means anything to him). After that we said our good-byes and went our separate ways.

I found Jerry who was just finishing up with his friends and asked him what he wanted to do now. He said that we had done enough for one trip; I had to agree as we did accomplish several things here this day, and we could come back again to check out the Center, as that was another place Jerry wanted to visit.

14

Galactic Federation

(1/29/2005)

I figured that I was about ready to look into the Galactic Federation. I stopped at Focus 21 and asked Jerry if he wanted to come along with me. He said, "Fine." So, we left Focus 21 and headed for Focus 27. Somewhere between Focus 24 and Focus 26 Jerry disappeared. I guess he got a better offer. I continued on alone. At the Library, I looked for Marty, but I was told he was not there today, so another Librarian came over to me and introduced himself as Abraham. I explained that I wanted to search out the Galactic Federation. "No problem, it is in the Science Department, right this way", he said. We entered the Science research room (the one with the glass windows where they do the research), and he brought over the file for the Galactic Federation. I thanked him and then sat down at the viewer to look at the file.

As soon as I opened the file, I physically got the sensation of far distance movement. In fact, the movement was so severe that I actually felt like I had to throw up. This had never happened to me before even though I had traveled back and forth in time. This was totally different and physical. I must have moved light years away from where I was, at least that is the perception I was getting, although I forgot to ask anyone our location in proximity of Earth. I was so taken by the motion sickness that I almost could not continue the voyage. Maybe that's why I don't like ocean cruises.

Anyway, when I finally slowed down to a stop, I was at some kind of building. I met someone who gave me their name, but I can't recall it. I explained why I was there, and I was told that I came at a good time. I said, "Really?" Strange how these things work out, isn't it? It turned out that they were having a discussion about Earth at that time in the Council Room. I was directed there and introduced to some people. They all welcomed me, which really surprised me as I was intruding on their discussions. They explained to me that they were in the discussion stages on whether or not this new device that they motioned to should be given to the people of Earth. I went over to the device and a person there explained what it was to me. This small suitcase-type device was a new power generator. I was asked, "Are you an engineer? " I said, "No, but my son was one." They told me to bring him next time. I said, "That might be hard." They replied, "No it isn't, you just bring him when he is asleep." Then it dawned on me, I could visit my kids, or anyone else, while they were asleep and I could interact with them. Although they may or may not remember it when they awaken. I remembered that Bruce Moen had done this with his own children, and they began to remember the trips. I made up my mind to definitely give this a try. (Especially my son, since he is very skeptical.) I asked,

"How much power can this produce?" I was told that this little generator could power New York City on Earth. I stated, "You have got to be kidding me." They assured me that it was true! I had to take them at their word, which considering where I was, was not too difficult to do.

I asked them what the discussions were about. They said that even though this generator could solve most of the world's energy problems, it could be used for destructive purposes too. I figured that there was a catch. At least someone is thinking about the technology that we have, and whether or not we should have it. I said, "This place is like a United Nations that really works!" They assured me that Earth had just recently been admitted to the Federation since we could now travel to this area by way of the subconscious. This was acknowledged as a big step in our evolution and that we should be congratulated for accessing these areas. I told them that I was not the first person to think of this and do it. I said, "I am just a beginning student in this nonphysical realm." They stated that that may be the case, but my being there said a lot about my development and about the Earth as a whole. I thanked them profusely for the compliment but reiterated that I was just a beginner at this. I did not want them to get the impression that I was somebody special.

I listened to some of the conversations, even though they were in totally foreign languages, but if I tuned into a conversation I could understand what was being said. Very cool! These conversations were very intense at times. Both sides seemed to be making good points. Then one of them turned to me and asked my opinion. I was astounded that they would even consider asking for my input. I was told that I was presently the representative from Earth at this meeting so that my input was not only wanted, but also necessary for the whole process. I said, "I would have to agree with the parties who say that we are too young for this type of energy system." I explained that in my opinion we would probably use it for destructive purposes at this time. I said, "Possibly before I pass from this lifetime, we may be ready for it as we are going in the direction away from destroying ourselves to one of preservation." I also remembered a quote from some television show. "The very young do not always listen." I had to admit that that was an appropriate comment on where the Earth fit into the scheme of things at this time. They thanked me for my input and continued on in their conversations. Either way that they were going to decide on this issue seemed to be a long way off. At least that was the impression that I was getting. So maybe, if they move like a large conglomerate, very slow in making any major decision, we may be ready for the power unit by that time. We'll just have to wait and see.

As it seemed that I was being pulled back from the meeting, I thanked everyone but told them that it was time for me to go. As I was leaving, the person over by the machine, said, "Bring your son next time". I told him that I would try, but could not guarantee it.

15

Exploring with the Kids

I tried a trip with my kids while they were sleeping at night. It was pretty good too. What I did was to pick them both up. My daughter was first so she could get her brother to come along for the ride. I used a beautiful purple magic carpet with golden fringes and designs on it. I explained to them what I was attempting to do and, of course, my son was skeptical. I told them that everything we do is going to be completely different from anything we would normally do, so that they might be able to remember it happening when they wake up.

I told them that we were going to take a trip to another part of the world. We were going to Peru, a place that neither would ever think about going to. I said since we were on a magic flying carpet we could view the Nazca Lines from above and then go down for a closer look. That is exactly what we did. I showed them several different shapes in the sand, which they thought were pretty cool. I told them that no one really knows why the people put these pictures here, but that it was apparent that they were to be viewed from the sky. I took them down to the ground so that they could get the perspective on how really big these pictures were. When we got down, my daughter said, "Where are they?" I replied, "Do you see this little indentation in the ground here? If you follow that you can see that it makes a picture, a huge picture." This brought home to them the idea of the large size of the pictures, and they could not believe how someone could make them on the ground without seeing the finished product. I told them I was glad to see that they were thinking about this, and why someone on the ground would do all this work when, at the time they made them, no one could fly.

When the ride was finished I told them that we still had time for another quick trip. I said, "How about a roller coaster ride?" I told them that would be something that would make an impression on them, and they might actually remember doing it too. They agreed. We went to Sandusky, Ohio, where they have huge roller coasters. We got on the biggest one we could find, and I told them to hang on tight. I was not really looking forward to the ride, but I figured that I had to stay with them for this adventure. We went up and up to the top and when we went over the top I was expecting to feel the fast acceleration and the butterflies in my stomach. But, I did not. Since I had earlier experienced the movement by going to the Federation I thought that I would feel similarly. But, I realized that things that happen on Earth, be they now or in the past, would be different. The Federation must be very far away from Earth, meaning that an actual physical and locative movement had to occur. I will make a note of that the next time I venture out into the Universe.

When the ride was finished, I told them that it was time to go but that we would do it again. I explained to them that

they should try to remember these events if they could and that
I would be back for others in the future. They said great. I told
them they could even get their own flying carpets next time if
they want to, my daughter said, "That would be so cool." I took
them back to their beds and left them.

16

Letter from Jerry about my Journeys

Rich,

Thanks so much for the latest adventure. It was by far the best and most complete. Your writing flows very well, and it is apparent that you are getting more comfortable with it. You may end up being quite a talented storyteller as this process unfolds. That will be great since I think there is at least one book in your future, if not more. I am very serious when I say this.

I do not have any conscious memory of our adventure, but I did go to Focus 27 on my own, or at least I thought I was on my own. I do have a Priest friend who is dead and with whom I visited briefly while there.

In my travels I meet up with a young Asian man with long, straight black hair. He wears a traditional oriental robe that is obviously of very good quality although it is not ornate. At times he is beside me and at other times he is me. I am not sure, at this point; exactly what the process is that is taking place.

While I was out I retrieved two individuals. One was an army airman from WWII and the other was a friend of mine who recently passed away. It is amazing that the situation seems more real to me as I think about it now than it did when I actually experienced it. Quite a bit of it happens more as feelings than as clear visual scenes. I do "see" but not in the conventional way.

The most interesting thing of all is that I have been working for months now visualizing a power source that is very small and very powerful that I can design and manufacture so that individuals like you and I can get off the grid and have virtually free energy to power our homes, autos, boats and eventually planes. I have been very serious and doing visualizations every day for months on this product. I have been having doubts about whether the government would ever allow it to be given to the general public, and keep putting that in Spirit's hands. I am also visualizing a computer program that will revolutionize that industry.

I wonder what the connection is between my visualizations and your visit to the Federation. How's that for Confirmation of one of your trips!

I am leaving at about two-thirty this afternoon for PA and will be away until late Tuesday afternoon. I am anxious to hear what you have to say about the stuff I have told you today!

Thanks again for the adventures. They made my day!!!

— Jerry

My Response:

Jerry,

Thanks for the vote of confidence in regard to my writing.

As far as you and I in Focus 27, I recall you visiting with the priests so we were at least together for part of the time. As far as your Oriental man in the robe goes, he could be other aspects of yourself, since you say that he is at times you and not you. There probably are parts of yourself that you have to get reacquainted with or heal in some way.

I am going to see "Indigo" the movie tonight. I could not get tickets for the theatre, but some organization is having it at their house. I can't wait to see it. You can go on the Internet and check if it will be in your area. I don't know why spiritual movies are so hard to find, like 'What the Bleep for example'. I know they may not be great moneymakers, but if more people knew they were in theatres, their attendance might be increased.

I agree with you that the experiences seem more real as time passes than they do when they actually occur. It seems almost like we're in a dream state while experiencing these events. But, I do recall from my past life regression hypnosis experiences that I was never deeply out of consciousness at the time. I'm sure I was almost totally awake during the whole process. These events now seem very similar to that feeling, since I can still delineate between what is going on in my mind and what is around me in the physical. We'll have to discuss this more when we get together.

As far as "seeing" these events, I agree with you that they do not always happen when you actually "see" them happening, they are more in my mind's eye or "third eye". However, sometimes I get full colors and textures of things, but not often. I guess we just have to accept what we get and be happy with it. I am so grateful that I can actually do some of these things. There is so much that I want to do that I can't wait for my next trip. I could just be out there all the time and enjoy these things. I have to be careful to not get too wrapped up because you can easily forget about the reality that we are currently in.

As far as your power generator goes, why don't you take a trip to the Federation and find out if the one I saw is similar to what you are working on? You can tell them that you have been working on it at your end and see what they say. I took my kids there last night so my son could talk to them about it. I doubt that he will remember, but I'll keep trying anyway. I don't know what they said to my son, but he was in conversations about it for a long time and my daughter was listening too. I'd love to have either of them remember these trips, but as long as I can go out there with them sometimes, I'm happy, it's just fun to take the trip.

I'll keep looking for you at the Café in Focus 21. Maybe we can start remembering the trips we do together. I'm glad to have a fellow explorer to share these with me. Keep me posted on your journeys.

—Rich

17

The Cosmos

(1/30/2005)

I decided to take a trip into the Cosmos and just go with the flow. However, please be careful if you do that!

I was not getting much action the last time or two when I tried to direct myself, so I figured that there was something else going on. To find out, I set my goals on nothing and just go with whatever came up. I asked my guides for help and, as usual, they came through with a vengeance. I was totally unprepared for what happened next.

I was out in Focus 27, but not at the Park. I was in deep space just wandering around when I definitely noticed a shift change in my perspective. I realized it was weird, but I went with it. I received the distinct impression that I was in Focus 29. I had never been there, and don't know anyone who had been, so I have no one I can compare notes with. I was in a higher level to be sure. I was searching around and asked for guidance and my answer came like a lightening bolt. My whole body started to vibrate uncontrollably. I was not frightened, but I could not control what was happening. I was told that

I had to get my physical body onto a higher plane so that I could communicate with higher entities. I was familiar with the fact that the higher levels require a phase shift in the physical body to access them. But, I was not looking to do that and was not expecting that to happen either! I could not directly communicate with anyone on this higher level, but I was told that I would be able to at some future date. I was also told that I would have to go through this process three different times to accomplish the vibrational change on my physical body. It was all right with me so they continued charging my body. My body went from very low vibrations to ones where I was literally shaking from head to toe. Very strange, but again I was not scared or frightened by the whole experience. I just went with the flow.

This continued to happen at repeated intervals of a few minutes each during this session. On one of the Going Home tapes they leave you out there and do not bring you back. I like these tapes because you can explore as long as you like without having to countdown back to consciousness. I have found no problem coming back whenever I wanted to. After this first session of vibrations, I took a long time to come back to my physical reality. I did not experience an Out of Body Experience (OBE)! My body just vibrated like hell. I took the time to enjoy what was happening because I knew that it was being done for a reason.

After this session, my body felt much energized. I was not tired, but I still had this tingling feeling throughout my body. I know that I will have to continue this two more times before I have completed the changes. I still don't know if I will then be able to contact someone on the higher levels, or if I will have to wait until the time is right for them to show themselves to me. I guess I have to go with their choices because I have nothing to do with what is happening.

18

Back to the Federation

(2/1/ 2005)

I started in Focus 21 at the Café. I looked for Jerry, but I guess he was out and about by himself as he was not there. What I found for the first time was the Bridge that everyone had been telling me about. My Bridge, as everyone has his or her own version, is a small bridge over a stream maybe twenty feet across. The Bridge itself is made entirely of oak. There is a high-gloss polyurethane varnish covering the entire length, which makes it really sparkle in the bright sunshine. This is the Bridge that I crossed over for the first time to go on from Focus 21.

As I made my way across the Bridge, I asked guidance if there was anyone at Focus 23 that needed my help. I slowed down passing through Focus 23 and looked around for anyone there. I sensed no one so I continued on. When I got to Focus 27 I said, "What should I do today?" I remembered that I wanted to take my son to the Federation, so I decided to do that. I went and picked him up without his sister. He was a little more receptive this time than last. I told him where we were going, and he seemed interested. We started by going back to the Library to pull out the Galactic Federation file to view on the screen. I realized that I could go there directly, but I decided to go through the Library with my son.

Next time I'll go direct. As I put the file into the viewer, I was again immediately hit by a moving sensation, but this time it was much gentler than the last. I did not get seasick or queasy. My son, Richie, had no problem with movement, as he always loved those rides at the shore that go round and round. I always hated them.

When we arrived at the Federation building, Richie thought that it was very impressive. It has a large entrance room that is at least 70-feet high with all glass and stainless steel pillars around. The room is expansive and there were many people having discussions, which made for a very noisy place. I remembered where we had to go from my last visit so we went directly there. I explained to Richie that these people wanted to show him this new generator design, but I could not understand the workings, but he might. As we approached the area with the generator, the same person that I met last trip was there as if waiting for us to arrive. He said, "Ah! I see you brought your son back this time". I said, "Yes, Richie might understand more than I could about the machine." I left him there to find out more about the generator, and I went back down the hall to visit with the people having discussions about giving the generator to the Earth. As I was proceeding back down the hall, I started to get pulled back to Focus 23. I sensed that I was needed there. I went back to my son and told him that I had to go do a retrieval, and I would try to return before he finished up. I asked him if he could get back home okay if I did not come back for him before he was finished. I was told that he would be taken care of. So off I went back to Focus 23, wondering why I was not stopped as I had passed through it before. No matter, I'll just go with the flow.

Upon arriving at Focus 23 I looked around and could not find anyone. I did not sense anyone either. It was very baffling to me. I searched some more, and I heard my name being called, yet I could not find anyone. I think that I was trying too hard, I have gotten that feeling before, and I know it well. We always want these things to flow smoothly and quickly as one expects in the physical, but in the non-physical there is no time or distance, so those parameters are not the same. I decided to not try so hard, but it is difficult. I know we have all experienced that in these realms. We want something to happen and try and try but it never seems to work. So we have to go back to the beginning and start again. Well, since I was already into this adventure and had to keep moving, I said to myself that I would stay a bit longer but then would leave to get back to my son. Sure enough, just when I decided that I had to go back and give up looking, I sensed someone nearby. Naturally, when we give up trying, these things always happen. I'm still working on this aspect of travel.

I looked around and saw an eleven-year old boy with a scuffed knee sitting alongside this road in the middle of some farmland with fields of hay all around. I went over to him and offered to help him. He said his name was Tommy. I asked, ""What's the matter?" He told me that he could not find his way home. So, I asked, "What was the last thing you remembered?" He said that he had been fishing down by a stream and he had fallen in. I said, "I guess that's where that scrape on your knee came from." He replied, "Yes." I told him that I could help him get to where there were people that he did know. At this time I did not tell him he was dead, so as not to scare him. He said that he would like that. I grabbed his hand and we started to rise up. MISTAKE! He let go of my hand, and he went back down to the ground looking frightened. I went back to him and apologized for not telling him we would be going up in the air. He said, "What the heck is going on? How can you fly?" I told him that he could fly now also, if he wanted to. He didn't understand, so I had to explain. I told him that he had drowned by the stream and that he was only a spirit now. Of course, he did not believe me. I told him to touch the telephone pole next to him. He tried to and his hand went right through it. He was flabbergasted, and he did it several more times to make sure that he wasn't seeing things. A short time later he stopped and just looked at me. I tried to be as gentle as I could, and I told him that he was only a spirit and that he no longer belonged in this earthbound reality. Then I asked him if there were any relatives that he had known who had passed on. He said, "My uncle Pete." Then he quickly said, "Oh and grandma." I asked him if he would like me to take him where they were because they were waiting for him. He was not sure if I was telling him the truth. I said, "Look, you have been here for awhile and no one else has helped you. I'm here to help you now, and if you don't like where I take you, you can always come back." That seemed to be fine with him. I took his hand and lifted off again. This time he was not as frightened, and he looked around the countryside from the height we were at, enjoying the view.

After a short time we arrived at the Park and we were walking along the path by the stream. I asked,"Tommy, how do you like the park?" He said that it was okay. Up ahead I saw two people standing waiting for us. I said, "Look up ahead, is that your Uncle and grandmother?" He became excited and said, "Yes." He ran over to them, and they hugged him and kissed him. It was a really nice reunion. I stopped over by them and they thanked me for bringing Tommy to them. I replied, "It was my pleasure."

I had to get back to the Federation to pick up my son. I refocused my energy to take me back to the Federation building and was quickly returned. I looked around and said, "Wow that was quick." I did not know how long I had been gone. I searched for my son, and he was just finishing up with the man about the generator. We thanked him for his help and started to return down the hall to the main gallery. I asked, "What did you learn?" He said that he could not believe all the things he had been told. I reminded him that he would probably not remember all of the information right now, but that at some future time he may be able to put it to good use. He was disappointed at that statement because he was so excited and wanted to use the information right now. I explained to him that it did not work that way. I said, "Many times we are given information and cannot access it consciously until we're supposed to. I can't tell you when that will be, but you'll be able to access the information when the time's right." I told him that maybe his dad is not nuts after all. He had to agree. Again, I told him that he would not remember this conversation either, but that I would keep trying, and I would take him on other adventures when the time was right. I dropped him off and returned myself.

19

Nothing Works

(2/2/2005)

I tried to go on a journey today but nothing happened. This happened last week too a couple of times. I had tried to go out and had no luck. It dawned on me that this might be some type of lesson to prove to me that when I do go on a journey it is really happening. If I go out sometimes and get nothing, that's fine too. But, when I go out and have an adventure, spirit is telling me it is for real. Just a thought that makes sense to me that I wanted to pass along because I know some of you are thinking that some of this stuff can't be real. Well, I'm the first to admit that I cannot guarantee its all real, as I am only telling you the things that I have perceived during my own adventures. This just puts a little more information on the side of leaning toward the reality of it all so you can see that when I write something, it is something that I feel I've experienced.

Anyway, during the episode this morning, I went back to the Cosmos and felt that I was again in Focus 29 beyond the Park. I got the impression that there were entities around me again, but I could not communicate with them. I experienced some more vibrational episodes. I do not think that I have raised my energy level high enough to actually communicate with these entities, so I will just have to keep trying.

20

Mount Rushmore

(2/3/2005)

I decided to take the kids out again for a trip. I picked them up on my flying carpet and took them to Mount Rushmore, and then to Devil's Tower in Wyoming. We had taken a cross-country trip several years ago but by taking them somewhere in the non-physical I thought I might impress them more. They really got a charge out of being able to go up to Washington's nose and touch the smooth rock. They did not realize that Roosevelt's eyeglasses were done in relief, and Lincoln's pupil in his eye was almost as tall as they were. After we had looked this monument over pretty well, I told them we were going to Devil's Tower. Arriving there and landing on the top was pretty neat, because you usually have to climb up and down to get to the top using ropes. They both like to rope climb, but I told them not today. This time we didn't need ropes.

I must have dropped them off, because the next thing I knew I was in Focus 23 walking down the hallway in a high school, and I saw a janitor on a ladder climbing up into the ceiling. I had a good idea what I was going to find. I walked over to the janitor and asked, "Do you need any help?" He came down from the ceiling and said, "Are you talking to me?" I said, "Yes." He told me that no one had been listening to him, and he was starting to get mad. I asked him what he meant. He said, "Well, the kids come down the hallway and just totally ignore me, as if I wasn't even there." I had to ask him what was the last thing he remembered. He told me that he was up in the ceiling and had lost his balance and fell, but he insisted that he was all right. I told him that was the problem, and he was not all right. I explained to him that he was no longer in the physical realm-- he had passed on to non-physical reality. Of course, he didn't believe me. I explained, "That was the reason no one pays attention to you, because they cannot hear you or see you anymore." He thought about this for a while. It did start to make sense to him, but he still did not believe me. I asked him to move the ladder from the middle of the hallway over to the side. He attempted to, but he could not grab it. I said, "See?" I told him that it was time to move on from here and decide what he wanted to do next. He wasn't sure what I meant by that. I explained that I could take him to the Park, meet some friends or relatives of his, and they would help him onto his next journey. He decided that he might as well come along since he was no longer doing any good around there. We made a quick trip to the Park and found his parents waiting for him. His father was dressed in his best Sunday suit and his mother had on a beautiful dress with printed flowers of various colors. They were very glad to meet again, and they thanked me for bringing their son back to them. I told them the pleasure was mine.

MOUNT RUSHMORE

(2 /4 /2005)

I have just been re-reading Bruce Moen's Book *Voyage Beyond Doubt*. I had wanted to read how he had gotten his children to explore with him again. I did not remember that his children were only four and nine at the time. I recalled from somewhere that children can experience these things much easier than adults, as their belief systems had not been polluted by life experiences, which tends to shut down our early beliefs, such as magic and flying.

Just a note here that I forgot to put in an earlier episode. One night when I went to pick up my son, with my daughter along, he woke up and looked at us, then went back to sleep. I wondered if he would remember that one. So I asked my daughter. She said that she did not remember the journey but that even if Richie did, he would never admit it to me. I said, "You're probably right." But, I could not believe it when it happened because I could see him wake up, look at us in our non-physical bodies and then lie back down and go back to sleep. He did come along in his non-physical body for the ride though, so he did not miss it.

Getting back to the book, Bruce goes into the fact that, even though he was experiencing these events in the non-physical, he still had a hard time believing that they were real. He discusses a time where he was with his travel partner, Rebecca, and he experienced a non-physical sense of smell in his physical body. Whereby his non-physical self experienced it (the smell) and brought the odor to his physical awareness, but as soon as he found out that the odor was from his non-physical side, he immediately stopped smelling this odor.

TALKING WITH ANGELS

After I read this I began to think of some of the problems that I have been having lately in regard to not always being able to either remember what was happening or to occasionally have an event happen. The thought occurred to me that I must have been having the same problem as Bruce. All of these things that are happening just do not make sense to the left-brain, logical mind that has to analyze everything for us. Now, it makes perfect sense to me. I, on one level experience these happenings, but on another level, my mind says that I am making it up. As I have previously stated, I cannot tell you that I know definitely these things happen when I travel, but in the past my mind has not been able to make up such strange adventures. What I am trying to convey here is that I am still struggling with the reality of these events. Sometimes I have no problem with it and enjoy the ride, and I get a lot accomplished; however, other times my left-brain must be too active and it shuts my perception down, even though I do not realize that it is happening. WAIT! I just had a thought to prevent this from happening. Since I know what is happening when it happens, I just have to give my left-brain something else to do so it does not interfere with my travels. I had done that a while back when I was having trouble getting to different Focus levels and it worked there. I will just have to do the same thing now and tell my left-brain to do something else; I can tell it to monitor my body for how it is feeling at whatever level I happen to be in, or area that I happen to be in, so that I can return there whenever I choose to. This has worked in the past, and I will try it again to see if it has an affect when I cannot perceive what I am trying to do. I believe that it will work.

21

Healing Temple

(2/7/2005)

Today I decided to take a trip wherever I needed to go and just let the Ether take me to a place that was entirely at random. I stopped at Focus 21 and Focus 23 going out just to check, but nothing much was happening there. I went on to Focus 27 and while I was looking around I did not feel attracted to any particular area. I just cleared my mind and made it a total white sheet with nothing on it. I saw this cowboy standing next to a wooden fence with a toothpick in his mouth; he just flashed by and was gone. I thought that was pretty weird. I was not getting any other info so I went back to the white sheet. Then, I saw a baseball come hurtling through the air right at my white sheet, hit it and roll off. This happened several times until I saw a boy with a baseball glove sitting at the bottom of the sheet laughing like crazy. I knew he was laughing at my perplexed look at what in the world was going on, but he just kept laughing and did not tell me anything else. This went on for a while and then I was pulled towards the back of the sheet, which I found to be very dark, and I was wondering what was happening. Suddenly, I felt movement and I knew I was traveling somewhere.

When I finally stopped, I was on this hill overlooking a very large expanse with rolling hills and trees. Off in the far distance I saw a glass-domed building, which was very large, and I asked my guide if that was where I was supposed to go. I was told, "Yes" and I took off walking towards this domed building. As I approached it, I began to realize the size of the building. It was huge, very tall and least 150-feet high and covered in glass and steel for support. It looked familiar, but I could not quite place it. Walking along an entrance path which was a wide dirt-path leading to a grand entrance, whom should come running out of the building but Dee! She was all excited that I was there and grabbed my arm and started to pull me into the building as fast as she could. I said, "What's going on?" She said, "I'll show you; just hurry up and get in here." I had no choice but to follow along as she pulled me into the building.

When we finally got inside the gallery area she at last slowed down a bit so I was not running to keep up with her. She said, "We have to go down this hallway over here." I looked, and I saw several hallways leading off of the main gallery area. I said "Which one?" She pointed and said, "This one" as if I should have known. It was a very long hallway that seemed to go on forever. We started down the hall together and after a short period of time Dee said, "In here". We entered a room, and I said, "What now?" The room looked like a doctor's treatment room where you could get a physical. I asked, "What are we doing here?" Dee answered, "This is the room where they do healings." I asked her who was going to be healed and she said, "You." I said, "I'm not

sick." Dee said that I had some physical problems that they were
going to take care of today. I have some physical problems, mainly
in my sinuses. I figured what the heck, if they can help, why not?
We waited for someone to come in. I clicked out after that, and I
don't know what happened.

Rich.

*This journey was a part of your vibrational shift. Not only did
you go through things that you experienced when you were twitch-
ing, etc. But, you also took multiple trips to the Healing Temple, and
usually don't remember them, or who is doing the healing. In actu-
ality it was a group of people...a spirit family or soul group, and was
usually a very ceremonial type of thing...but different, depending on
whose eyes it is seen from. I know that you know what I am talking
about. It is so funny that this happened because this morning I had
said to my Angels, "Let's go have a journey with Rich, okay?"*

Dee

22

Brothers

(2/9/2005)

I started at Focus 21, greeted everyone, but no one wanted to come along for a journey so I went across the Bridge to Focus 23 by myself, opened up my awareness all around me, but did not feel pulled in any one direction, so I continued on to Focus 27. Arriving in Focus 27 and walking along the stream, a young boy came up beside me and started walking with me. He did not say anything, but I figured that since he was there with me he wanted to talk to me. I said, "How can I help you?" He said that he needed my help for his brother. We sat down on the wall along the stream, and he told me his story. It seemed that his brother had died in a plane crash but was still stuck at the plane. He had not moved on from it, and his little brother could not get his attention. So, the little boy, Bruce, asked me if I could help him out. I said, "Of course, I would be happy to." We ventured back to Focus 23 and found Bruce's brother, Andy, still sitting in his seat on the plane. Bruce said, "There he is, that's the way I always see him, and he does not see me." I told Bruce that we could help his brother to move on from here. We went over and sat right in front of Andy, and I got his attention. I said to Andy, "What are you doing here?" Andy said that he knew the plane was going to crash, and he was waiting for it to happen. I explained to him that the plane had already crashed and that he had died as a result. It did not seem to register with him, as he was still focused on the pre-crash aspect of it happening. I tried again to explain what happened and I told him that I had his brother, Bruce, with me to help him. He said, "That's impossible since Bruce died in a drowning accident many years before." I told him that Bruce was there with me to help guide him to his next life. He still could not see Bruce. I asked him to put out his hand, and I would have Bruce grab it, and he should feel the connection. As he did this, Bruce grabbed his brother's hand and held on tight. Andy seemed to feel it, and slowly Bruce started to come into his awareness. As this happened, Andy began to look more at ease with the situation. Bruce then gave him a big hug and the two of them were now feeling a bit relieved. I asked them if they wanted to proceed with me to the Park. Bruce said,

"That's all right, I can take Andy along to the Park." I guess he felt proud that he was going to show his big brother something. They both drifted off on their own to Focus 27.

Since I was still at the crash site, I figured that there was at least one other person in need of help. It didn't take long to find her. The stewardess was lying in the aisle. I walked over to her and tried to help her up off of the floor. She expressed her thanks and said, "We have to help these people." I explained that the plane had crashed and that she had died along with many others. She was not comfortable with that explanation until she looked around and did not see anyone else. She said that her name was Angie. I heard someone moaning a little farther back in the plane so we went down the aisle to take a look. We found a man with a seat crushed up against him. He was trying to get out from beneath it. I told him that we would help. I moved over to him and pulled the seat off of him. He was able to squeeze out from underneath, and he thanked me profusely. He had an injured arm, so I told him that I could take him to a place to get it fixed. Angie was still standing there trying to get her bearings on what was happening. I did my best to explain to the two of them that the plane had crashed and that they had both died. I said that I could take them both to the Park where they could get help and meet others that they knew. I asked them both if they had friends or relatives that had passed that they would like to see again. The man said that he had a brother and a cousin that he would like to see, but not really believing me though. That was the impression that I got from him. Angie said that she would like to meet her father. So I told them that I would honor both of their requests and that there would be a medical facility for the man to get his arm attended to. We took off from the crash site and floated into Focus 27. There, as I had promised was the man's brother and cousin waiting for him. There was also an ambulance with paramedics waiting to treat his injury. Angie's dad was there too. As they both walked over to their respective relatives, I felt a sense of pride that I had been able to assist them in their time of need.

Not having anything else going on then, I decided to go to the Library and look up another of my past lives. While looking through the archives on myself, the year 1928 jumped out at me.

I said, "I guess this is where I was to go today." Pulling out the file and placing it in the viewer, the first thing I saw was a beautiful brand new Packard car sitting in the sun. It was a dark-green convertible and a beautiful automobile. Looking around I found that I was there as a young and handsome man in his late twenties. I could tell that he was a privileged person by the car and by the way he was dressed. He (I) had on a button-down shirt with a cardigan sweater, fancy shoes, socks that came up from the ankle to below the knee, and those baggy pants, whatever they were called, like golfing pants I guess. He looked very dapper, and I was a bit jealous of the way he looked. He seemed to be really enjoying life. I guess sometimes we get it all, and other times we get what we get. Anyway, unfortunately this was not to last very long. The next impression I got was that he was in a car crash, probably due to his own inattention to the road. He had been thrown from the car and died. So I guess when we think that we have it all, sometimes it can be very fleeting.

That was the end of that adventure. However, I forgot to write down this one from the other day. I decided to go out into the Ether with my friend Gary. He had always told me that when I was able to start traveling the Ether that I should pick him up and we would go on a trip. He said he would try to remember me getting him. I took off for his house and had to wake him up. He did not want to wake up, but when I told him that we were going on an adventure, he perked right up. I said that I would take him to the Library and go to the Unwritten History section. I decided that we were going to look for the Ark of the Covenant. He said, "That would be a terrific place to go." We found the file in the Library and placed it in the viewer. Immediately we were transported through time. I was used to this by now so it did not bother me, but Gary had to get his "sea" legs. He was a little unsure of himself for a while. When we stopped, we were inside a dark tunnel. I asked my guide if we were in the right place, and I was assured that we were. We walked along this tunnel and finally came to a large room that was made of old stone and peaked in a dome overhead that was about twenty-feet up. But, there was nothing in the room. I thought that maybe we were in the wrong time. As I thought that, guidance was there with a little push, and I noticed another room (like an anti-room) off to one corner. I said that that was probably the place we should be. We went over there and were able to gain access to the anti-room. As we entered, we were hit with a dazzling golden-light that was coming off a box in the middle of the room. It took awhile for our eyes to adjust to the brilliance of the room. I said, "This must be it!" Gary agreed. At first we could not tell how large it was due to the bright light. I asked guidance if anything could be done about the brightness of the light and as soon as I focused my attention on it, the light became much more bearable. This being accomplished, we could begin to really see what we were looking at. We were dumbstruck and the shear size and beauty of the Ark. It was made of gold with many decorations all around it. There were two large poles going across the top for carrying the Ark when necessary. The top had many Angel decorations and was just glorious. It had to be the most beautiful object that I have ever seen. I tried to get a feel for a time frame, and it felt like about 2,300 years ago, which would place it in about 300 B.C. We saw no one else around it at the time of our visit. We stayed for a short while just admiring it and soaking up the energy that was given off from it. The Ark is an unbelievably powerful energy source. After just being dazed by it for a while, we took our leave. I took Gary back home and told him that I hope he remembers the trip. That's why I chose such an outstanding item to show him, so that he would possibly remember it when he awoke.

23

Travel Without Hemi-Sync

Today I decided to take the plunge and travel without Hemi-Sync. I could not sleep tonight so I figured that I must have to travel somewhere. I didn't feel like getting up to get my tape recorder so I decided to try flying solo. As soon as I said that to myself and tried to clear my mind, I was instantly transported to this golf course like place. And, to my great surprise, I saw a person sitting in a purple open-cab dune buggy. She had on a gray-fur top hat with a black band around it, and those round-rimmed dark sunglasses like the hippies used to wear. She looked at me over the sunglasses and said, "Let's Go". I got into the dune buggy, and we were traveling for quite awhile. I asked, "Where are we going?" She said that we were almost there. We pulled up in front of an elevator that was standing in the middle of the golf course. I was told to get out, and she took off. I asked, "Are you coming with me? She said, "No, I'm just dropping you off." She then said, "107." I didn't quite understand what she said, and she repeated, "107." Not knowing what 107 was, I entered the elevator. Sure enough on the top of the buttons was Floor 107. So I pushed it. I did not get a sensation of movement, but when the doors opened, I was standing in an area that reminded me of the Park. I got out and started to walk across this plane and shortly I came to my familiar stream in the Park. I said to myself, "Well, that was an interesting way to get to the Park." As I was walking along the stream, I heard someone calling, "Dad, Dad wait up." I looked around and there was my daughter, Christine. I said, "What are you doing here?" She said, "I wanted to come with you on another trip." I said, "Fine, but how did you know how to find me?" I always went to pick her up and drop her off back at school. She said, "It was easy. All I did was set my sites on finding you and here you were." This was totally unexpected, and I could not believe that she was really there on her own. I guess that my other trips with her made an impression even though she did not consciously remember them. The mind is a very powerful tool that we can use in many ways. I was truly astounded that this could happen.

I said to Chris that since she wanted to come along, she gets to choose where we go. I asked, "Where do you want to go to-day?" She said, "The moon." I told her that it was no problem even though I had not gone to explore it myself. So I took her hand, told her to close her eyes, and I focused on being on the moon. We arrived shortly thereafter and started to explore. I can still feel the gray, powdery sand-like material that covers the surface. I picked some up and ran it through my hands. It was a very-fine powdery sand that tended to stick to you when you handled it. But it flowed right through my fingers like grains of sand on Earth. We looked around at several craters and saw some of the equipment left from the Apollo flights up there. Chris said that one of the craters looked like the one in Arizona that we had visited several years ago. We went down into the crater and looked up at the high walls all around us. It was a pretty breathtaking site to behold, as the craters on the moon are usually larger and deeper than those found on Earth. From our vantage point, at the bottom, I felt like a Lilliputian in *Gulliver's Travels* because we were so insignificant in the scheme of things. I said, "Let's take a look at the other side, the dark side of the moon." I understood that we don't see that side from Earth so I figured we should at least take a look while we were here. We went to the backside of the moon and found it to be somewhat similar to the front side. There was no light so it made it impossible to see the whole picture. I must have clicked out right about then because the next thing I knew I was back at the Library by myself. I didn't know what had happened to Chris, but I figured if she found her way there, she could find her way back home. Therefore, I did not worry about her.

Since I was alone now I decided to go into the Library and look at some more of my own history. I pulled a file that said 1625. I opened it up on the viewer and was immediately transported to Massachusetts in 1625. I was a Pilgrim and taking care of a farm. I had planted corn and tobacco. I don't know if tobacco can grow in that climate, but I guess no one was around to tell me I could not. I did not find out if the tobacco was harvested that year as I once again found myself back at the Library. I inquired what was going on, but my guide was mute on this question. I guess I just had to go with the flow. I still felt like I needed to do something else on this trip so I headed back into the Library and back to my file.

I had always had more problems with the left side of my body than the right side, so I asked my guide to take me to a place in my past where I could get an answer to why this was so. I pulled out 1695 or 1697, I forget which. I found myself on the roof of a tall building doing some repairs. It must have been twenty-five or thirty feet high. I lost my footing and fell off of the roof and landed on my left side. I was hurt very badly and really should not have survived the fall at all, especially since it was the late 1600's. I know that it took six-months to a year after that before I was able to get around. I used a cane and was not healthy the rest of my life. But, the most fascinating part of that little story was that my wife in that lifetime, who took very good care of me during my convalescence, seemed very familiar to me, but I could not quite place her. Afterwards, I sent this story to some friends, and it turned out that Dee said that the Angels told her that she was the one who took care of me in that lifetime, although she did not remember it either. Very interesting the way we learn things about our past selves and who we have spent time with before. I never get tired of exploring these areas and look forward to each and every new adventure on the other side of the veil.

(2/13/2005)

I met up with Thomas at the Café in Focus 21. He said that we had something we had to do. We headed out over the Bridge to Focus 27, but we breezed right through Focus 27 and went directly to Focus 29. Focus 29 is much different than lower levels because in Focus 29 you no longer have any kind of physical appearance. You are only light energy. I am trying to remember this as I had the experience this morning, but I am not writing it until late at night. I'll have to remember to write these earlier so I do not forget what has happened. Maybe I'll have to go back and revisit before I write about it. That may be difficult since my daughter wants to test out the validity of these experiments by doing something tonight in her dormitory room, and she asked me to try to observe whatever she has done when I go to pick her up for an adventure. I told her that I would try, but it does not always work exactly like that. Well, I can only write what I remember and if other items come to me at a later time, I will tell you where they belong.

I know Thomas was relaying some information to me, but I do not remember what it was. I do know that I experienced more vibrational tuning during this adventure and that we were brought into yet another Focus level. Thomas said to follow him, so I did. We then were at TMI There (similar to TMI on Earth) and descended to the Earth's Core Crystal. I had never been there and it was a truly different experience descending to the center of the Earth. Seeing the Crystal was an amazing occurrence. I had read about it, but actually being there, seeing it, and touching it, was altogether different. The Crystal is smooth and is supposed to be made of iron, but it looks like black malachite and is very shiny. When you touch it and run your hands over the surface you can feel the energy that it is giving off. Very powerful! I asked Thomas why we were there, and he said that I needed to get energy from the Crystal so that we could continue where were going. I gathered up as much energy from the Crystal I could reasonably obtain, and we moved on.

This was Focus 35, although I do not know how I knew that; I just felt that we were brought to Focus 35 by the change in my vibrational level. This was an area where we ran into the beings that Bruce Moen talked about in one of his books. There were beings interacting with humans on Earth, more observing than interacting really. They seemed to be observing what was going on but did not direct any actions. This is where I must have clicked out, because I do not remember anymore of this outing with Thomas.

24

Out of Phase

(2/19/2005)

I have spoken to several people this week, and it seems that Spirit is out of sorts. Everyone seems to be experiencing out of phase states where nothing is as it should be. Trying to focus on work related details seems to be all but impossible. I don't know if the planets are out of alignment, or exactly what the problem is, but energies are very weak and out of phase. So, my travels have been disrupted with me clicking out quite often and at other times I'd remember only parts of what happened for very brief periods of time. I do recall going back to Focus 29 a few times but beyond that I could not recall anything. I tried the lower levels of Focus 23 and Focus 27 several times but there was not much happening. I do recall getting pulled back to Focus 23 one time, but I clicked out right after I got there and, when I came back, I was already in Focus 24, by-passing Focus 23 altogether. Very strange energies to be sure.

This past week, the mother-in-law of a friend of mine passed over. I went to the funeral and was able to see lots of people that I have not seen in many years. As we grow older we seem to meet people at weddings and funerals, but I guess that is the way life is for most of us; we do not make the time to see the important people around us as often as we should. I had known her for most of my life as we all had grown up together since grade school, so I felt an additional pull to attend the funeral as well as the viewing.

While we were in church and one of the grand children was speaking about their grandmother, I got the urge to check on her to see if she was with us. I closed my eyes and drifted to a Focus level, which one I could not say, but as I opened my awareness I could see the woman who had passed and her husband sitting in the church next to me. I knew I had left room at the end of the aisle for some reason. As I focused my attention on them, she turned to me and acknowledged my seeing her. Then, she went back and focused on her granddaughter who was speaking in great detail about the many times they had shared together. I figured that she would be there since she was a very loving person, but I was not expecting her husband who had passed many years before. Since they were together I figured that she was fine on the other side and would not need my assistance in figuring things out.

I was going to leave it at that, but at the repast, my friend's daughter came over to me and asked me if I would check on her grandmother to be sure she was okay because she felt her grandmother would need some help. I told her I did check on her at church, and that she was there with her grandfather, but that I would check on her again just the same.

I started in Focus 21 and met up with Jerry, and I asked him if he wanted to come along. He said, "Sure." We both crossed the Bridge into Focus 23 although I knew she would not be there. Somewhere I lost Jerry again, as he seems to be very attached to Focus 25. I went to the Park to look around for her, but I did not feel her presence there either. I kept looking around. I was just about to give up and try again at another time when, as usually happens when one is about to give up from trying too hard, I was pulled to Focus 29. Now, when I say pulled, I mean that I was taken there by no choice of my own. I felt this swoosh of movement and was there in no time! I regained my thought process and began to look around in Focus 29. Please remember that Focus 29 is a state where there is no physical body, you are just light energy. I suppose it is not uncommon for people to go directly to Focus 29 after passing, but it was my first experience with this since I had not been there too often myself, due to the higher vibration level that one must be on in order to perceive there. It just struck me that maybe this is why I was given the ability recently to gain access to Focus 29 by making my own vibrational state that much higher.

Looking around I felt Teresa's (grandmother's) presence. She was there with her husband and was extremely happy to be with him again. As I stated Focus 29 is a light energy only Focus level, so I could not see her physical body since it had already been shed and just her light energy was visible. She knew why I had come, and when I started to tell her that I was just about to leave Focus 27 because I did not feel her presence, she stopped me and said that was the reason she pulled me to Focus 29. She said that she wanted everyone to know that she was fine. I would have to say fine indeed. To be in Focus 29 so quickly after passing from the Physical Realm you would have to be much more than fine. I asked her if there was any message that she wanted someone to know. She said," Nothing in particular." Apparently she had been able to settle everything while in the physical so she did not have any unfinished business to address. At that point, her husband stepped in and told me to pass along to Dennis that he should be very careful with the details of some type of negotiation that he was currently, or soon to be, involved with. I don't know if it was personal or business. Then, Teresa said to tell the girls to "Squeeze the bread". As there was nothing further to discuss, we said our goodbyes, and I thanked them both for meeting with me.

While returning from this journey it occurred to me that these journeys are never what one would expect. How one can be called to a higher level was really something that I never even thought could happen. Many terrific things can happen out in the Ether, and I intend to explore many more areas before I'm through.

25

Apple Pie

(2/22/2005)

This morning my journey took me directly to Focus 23 even as I just closed my eyes and started my tape. I still use tapes most of the time because the sounds direct me more quickly. At Focus 23 I saw this woman in a print dress sitting in a cushioned chair with a reading light to one side. There was someone else there trying to communicate with her but they were not getting through. The second person turned to me and said, "I'm glad you're here. I have been trying to get through to her, and she cannot hear me." I asked, "What was her name?" and I was told. "Martha." I said, "Martha can you here me?" She looked over at my direction but then turned away. At least I knew she could hear me. I asked the other person what had happened and was told that Martha had died peacefully, but could not accept that fact. I tried to get Martha to understand her new surroundings, but she seemed oblivious even to me. As I was explaining things, Dee showed up. I said, "You again?" She replied, "Yeah, I just came along for the ride." I said, "Good I could use some help." I explained to Dee what had happened, and asked her "Do you have any ideas on how to help in this situation?" Dee immediately said she always liked to bake apple pies. I did not understand, but it seemed to get Martha's attention. She smiled and said, "I always liked to bake too." So Dee said, "Come on, we'll go in the kitchen and bake one." Martha then got up off the chair and followed Dee to the kitchen. They were there talking pie recipes when Martha said that she had a friend who she used to cook with all the time. That was my queue. I asked, "Martha, would you like to see your friend again. She said, "I would." I said that we could all go and see her right now if she would like to. Martha loved that idea, so we left the kitchen and proceeded to Focus 27 and, sure enough, Martha's friend was there waiting for us. She was very happy to see her friend and the two of them just walked off together chatting away.

I said, "That was easy." Dee was still with me, and I asked her what she wanted to do. Dee said, "Let's go to the Temple." I said, "Fine" because I had no place that I was being drawn to at the time. We went to the Temple and were escorted to a healing room. Dee said we both need some healing. I knew that I could use some healing so I said, "Great idea." After we both had some healing done, I asked Dee what she wanted to do next. She said that she had nothing important to do. So, I asked her what was happening with the general vibrations going on in the world and when things would be changing again. She was not sure, but she said, "One more week." I said, "I can wait one more week." After that I clicked out, and Dee was gone when I returned, so I do not know what else transpired. However, it was interesting this time out. I sent Dee a copy of this journey.

APPLE PIE

Here is her response.

Rich

You know it is not a coincidence because I love to bake, and I have always been known for my apple pies (just ask my son) as well as my cooking. Anyway, that was pretty cool. Do you know whom the other person was that ended up helping out, besides Martha?

Dee

26

Sparkie

(3/1/2005)

I had an interesting adventure today. When I first went to Focus 23 I found a young woman searching around with a flashlight. I asked, "What are you doing?" She said, "It's so dark in here. Can you find the light switch?" So I just brightened the room up with my thoughts. She immediately said, "How did you do that?" I told her that she could do it too if she wanted to, but she didn't believe me. So as not to get hung up with all the explanations at that point I asked her how she had gotten here. She could not remember. Then, I said, "What is the last thing that you remember?" She said that she had been skiing and then she was here. This seemed a bit strange to me as she was wearing a white sleeveless top and black bell-bottom pants with boots, so it did not seem to me that she had been skiing, but I went along with her. I explained to her that she had possibly passed over due to a skiing accident, and she said, "Come on! You're kidding me, right?" I said, " No, it was not a joke and you have crossed over to the nonphysical." She said, "Okay, what do I do now?" I told her that she could do anything she chose to do, and I asked her if she had any relatives that she might want to see. She answered, "No, just my dog, Sparkie." I said that we could go see him right now if she liked, and she agreed. I took her hand and off we went to Focus 27. As we were walking by the stream I heard a barking sound and, sure enough, her dog came running over to her. She was very happy with that, and then some other people who apparently knew her too came over to greet her. She was delighted to see them all. They took her off with them, and they drifted away. It turned out to be a simple retrieval but I had initially thought it might be a tough one to handle.

I decided that since I was at the Center, I would look around inside of it since I had not done that. I went in the front door and looked around. I spotted a staircase to the second floor and was drawn to it. I walked up the stairs and it turned into a spiral staircase that kept on going. I thought, "How much higher does this go?" I received my answer from my guide. He said, "Not too much further". When I reached the top of the stairway I found an ordinary looking door, and I opened it and went in. There was no writing or indication as to what might be on the other side of that door, but I knew I was drawn there so there was something I needed to know on the other side. Upon opening the door, I found an office with a desk. I looked around for someone and called out, "Hello", but I did not receive any reply. I asked my guide for his advice and he said, "Wait". I never argue with my guide so that was what I did. A short time later a large turkey appeared out of no-where in the room and it jumped up on the desk. The turkey just sat there and looked at me and I looked at it. Then I said, "What now?" There was no answer. I sat a while longer and nothing else happened. I was getting a little upset at this uneventful situation, and I asked Dee to come and join me and we would go on a trip together. As soon as I said that, Dee showed up and asked, "Where do you want to go?"

I asked her if she had ever been to the Earth Core Crystal, and she said, " No." I told her that there was a giant crystal deep inside the Earth and that we could access it together, but first we had to make a stop at TMI to gather up some love energy to take with us as that was the proper procedure for going to the Crystal. I explained TMI There was just the same as TMI on Earth except that the Crystal, instead of being outside, was inside. So, off we went.

When we arrived at TMI There and were standing next to the Crystal gathering up Love energy, we also got wrapped up in the power of the Crystal. I knew that this kind of energy came off of the Crystal, but I had never experienced it for myself. We proceeded to go down and give the Earth Core Crystal all of the love that we had brought for it. The Crystal brightened appreciably when we were giving over our love energy. When we were done, Dee said, "Let's do that again." I agreed, and we went back to TMI There and to the Crystal and soaked up as much love energy that we could. After having visited the Earth Core Crystal a second time, Dee wanted to go one more time.

I said that this was the last time that we could go to the Earth Core Crystal and give it our love energy. However, when we threw our love energy onto the Earth Core Crystal for the third time it began to vibrate and shake to a small degree and it brightened ever so much more than the other previous two times. After that experience we returned and we each went our own way.

27

Pirates

(3/6/2005)

A friend of mine had been bugging me to take him out into the Ether and check on his past lives. I picked him up at his house and we went to the Library together. Unfortunately, he does not remember any of this happening, but that is usually the case. At the Library I took him to the past lives area and found his file. I told him to pick out any date he felt drawn too. He picked one out that simply said "1400", and we put his file onto the screening machine and looked at his life in and around 1400.

Apparently he was on a ship working as a carpenter, which is surprising to me because he knows nothing about carpentry or anything similar in this life. As we were looking around the ship, we learned that this was not just any ship but this was a pirate ship, or a Privateer, as they were originally called. When they first started out they were granted freedom of the seas and were usually working for one king who was at war with another, and they would raid the enemy's ships and make off with the spoils for their king. After awhile these Privateers stopped giving any to the King and just kept it for themselves. This is when the term

"Pirates" came to be used.

We also found out that my friend liked the ladies so much that he would be more interested in them when they were taken aboard a ship than he was interested in any spoils that had been gathered. Unfortunately, this lead him to contract one of the many diseases of the day and his pirate days were short lived. I clicked out after this.

(3/7/2005)

When I arrived at Focus 23 this day I looked around as usual but did not feel pulled to any place in particular, so I continued on to Focuses 24 to 26. Somewhere along there I was pulled back to Focus 23. I looked around for someone but did not see anyone until I turned around. When I did, I came face to face with a circus clown. He was fully dressed in a clown suit, and he had a big red nose that was an inch from my face. I was startled since I was not expecting this. I greeted him, moving a few feet back from where we were standing, and I asked, "Do you need any help?" He did not know what had happened to him, so I asked. "What was it that you last remembered?" He said that he was at the circus performing and then ended up here. I had to explain to him what had happened, and he took it pretty good-naturedly, but I could tell he thought that I was trying to put one over on him. I asked, "Is there someone you would like to see again on this side of the nonphysical?" He said that there were a few people that he would like to see again. I told him to come with me, and I'd take him to see these people right now. Again, I could tell he did not believe me, but he came along just the same. I think the reason he came along with me was because he no longer wanted to be by himself. He followed me. I knew there would be several people that he knew waiting for him upon our arrival. They all greeted him very excitedly, and he went on with them.

I have to say, that my retrievals have been mostly easy since I get the people to follow me, but I know there is someone waiting for me that will be a real challenge.

28

Dad

(3/9/2005)

I finished with a short trip today, which was different than any of those that I have had before. As I entered Focus 27 I asked guidance to take me where I needed to be. You have to be ready when you give this kind of idea to guidance because they usually take it and run with it, so be careful if you do this yourself. I received a one-word answer, "Emotions." I had a pretty good idea what guidance meant and went along for the ride.

Sensing something behind me, I turned around and what do you think I found? I saw all of the people that I have known throughout my life who have passed over to the other side! This is a pretty dramatic event, especially when you are not ready for it. I had somehow sensed that something like this would occur so I was not totally off guard when they all appeared. There were aunts and uncles and grandparents and friends. The one person that I wanted to see was there too, which made it all worthwhile --my dad. He had passed when I was twelve so I hadn't seen him in quite a while. We were both glad to see each other. He said, "I've been watching over you all this while and you're doing fine on most fronts." I asked him if he had seen my children (his grand children), and he seemed to burst with pride when I mentioned them. I said, "I was very proud of their accomplishments also."

We spoke at length, and he surprised me at all the things he knew about my life. I guess I should not have been surprised, but I was nevertheless. I said that I was currently at a turning point in my life and asked him if he could tell me in which direction to go. He smiled and said that he could not tell me what to do, as that choice was up to me. However, he did say that I was on a good path that will take me places that I haven't been to before. That was very cryptic and not very enlightening, unfortunately. He did, however, tell me that the path that I was on is a good one, and that I should continue to follow it. I said, "Thanks for the input", and I asked him to look in on my children and me every so often. He said he does... every day.

I thanked him again and told him that I would talk to him more often than I have. He said that was a good idea. I also said my goodbyes to everyone there.

29

Ladies Shoes

(3/14/2005)

I was out in Focus 27 with nothing really happening so I decided to take a look in on Jesus Christ. I adjusted my senses to find myself on a large rock in an arid environment. I looked around and there was Christ talking to a group of about twenty people. I started to venture over to them, and Christ looked at me and began to shake His finger in a "No" motion. I immediately got the impression that I was being told that this was not where I was supposed to be. So I came back to Focus 27 to see where I should be. Nothing much was there, and I was not being pulled anywhere. I thought that I should be somewhere because I was told to leave one area and I figured that I would see where to go. But since this was not the case, I said to myself "Just stop trying so hard." I know we all have been there. When I emptied my mind of thought, not too hard to do sometimes, I found myself in a room with these little tiny balls just buzzing around in one corner. I was then hit with the impression that these were all living souls that were waiting their turn to be placed back in a physical body, to be born again! I thought that was pretty neat. But, then

I clicked out. I guess I was not supposed to know much more about that aspect of our souls until some other time.

(3/17/2005)

Today's trip started at Focus 23. I was looking around and I saw a pair of ladies shoes, actually old-lady shoes, the kind your grandmother would wear that have a one-inch heel on them. Anyway, all I could see were the shoes and about one foot above them; I could not see the rest of the person's body. I had a feeling that I knew this person and the shoes looked familiar. I asked this person if I could help them, and she said that she did not know where she was and "Could I help her to find out what was going on?" I asked her what she last remembered, and she said she was sitting at the kitchen table and then ended up here. This sounded too familiar, but I could not put my finger on it at the time. I explained to her that she must have passed on while she was at the table.

She said that she couldn't be dead because she knows that when she dies the Angel Gabriel and a trumpet will meet her in Heaven! This was a little bit much for me to take because she said it like she demanded it to be that way. I saw that I was dealing with a person of very strong faith. But, I knew if I could get her to come with me to Focus 27, Gabriel would be there with the trumpet for her. I told her that I could take her to where she would meet Gabriel and others that she knew, if she would come along with me. Again I had this feeling of familiarity, and when she grabbed my outstretched hand, although I could not see hers,

LADIES SHOES

I felt it clasp around mine and off we went to Focus 27. When she grabbed my hand I knew where I had seen this person before, but I did not tell her that at the time. This woman was "me" in a previous lifetime! I knew that because of the shoes. I had seen her during a past life regression that I had done many years ago. All I knew of her was that she lived in the 1920's or 1930's, and I remembered this little old lady (a grandmother type of person), standing in her little kitchen, which would be fitting for the times. She had on an apron and a grandmother type of dress and those "shoes" that looked so familiar to me.

We arrived at Focus 27 along the path by the stream and sure enough there was Gabriel with the horn and some other Angels around for affect. This is what she was waiting for! And they put on the whole show that she was expecting; crafty fellows aren't they? They know exactly what people need at this stage of their journey. Her name was announced as we arrived; although I knew it then I cannot remember it now. She was greeted like royalty. Many of her friends were there and came over to greet her too. I stood back to watch this and all of a sudden as she was walking away, her whole body came into view for me to see. However, I only saw her from the back; I did not see her face. I guess Spirit didn't want me to become too familiar with her before I had done what I was supposed to do, which was bring her there. When I saw the whole person, even though it was from the back, I realized that this person was a lost aspect of myself. Maybe my feminine side. I'm not sure what part of me she was, but she was definitely part of me. After that I clicked out.

TALKING WITH ANGELS

(3/22/2005)

I was looking around in Focus 24 after having been immediately taken directly there. I knew someone was there that needed help, and I found him quite easily. He was about six-foot six and weighed at least five hundred pounds. Since I knew I was in Focus 24, I felt it quite certainly. This was a rather new experience, as I had not been taken directly to Focus 24 before, and I knew somehow that there was something different going on. I found this to be true. I asked the man, "Do you need help?" He said that he knew that he had died, but he was confused as to what was now happening. I could sense off in the distance other people present but not quite visible to me or to this person. Being in Focus 24 and knowing something specific should be happening here, I asked the man what religion he was. I was taken aback a bit when he said, "Buddhist." I should not have been surprised; it's just that this huge man did not strike my conscious mind as a Buddhist. But that was my own shortfall, not his. Now that I knew his religion, I figured that we were in the right place. I had felt the presence of other people. Since I knew what was happening, I asked the man what he was expecting to find here. He said that Buddha and other Buddhist priests should greet him as he had been taught. So I gently said to him that they were all waiting for his arrival, and if he would just open up his spirit to them, he would be able to see and hear them all. He said that he had been looking, but could not find anyone except me. I explained to him that he may be trying too hard to see and hear them and that this was preventing their getting through to him. I told him to "Relax and close your eyes and try to meditate and concentrate on the priests that you thought you should find here." He closed his eyes and began to chant. In a few moments I felt a presence in the room move over to where we were, and they came into view for me. I said, "You should now open your eyes and see who was here for you." He was very surprised to see not only the priests and monks that he thought would be there, but also some relatives that he was not expecting to see. This became a very cordial scene and they thanked me for my help. I said, " It was my pleasure to afford my help to them."

30

The Beige Blanket

(3/30/2005)

The next time out in the Ether I found myself driving down a road with Dee, and we saw an accident. We stopped and saw that there were people all around. Many of them apparently had died and were walking around in a daze. We both took off in different directions to help anyone we could. I found several people that were together so I walked over to them and showed them how to go to the Light, which was a short distance from where we were standing. They all very naturally drifted over to the Light and were immediately taken care of by other helpers. Then, I found three family members grieving over someone whom they had lost. They said that the body was in a makeshift morgue off to the side of where they were sitting. I went over to this area and found a body covered with a beige blanket. This whole experience was the first time that I had the experience of full-blown three-dimensional color with feeling and textures. It was a new experience for me. In the past I had perceived these things, and they became more understandable when I wrote them down, but this was the first time I had seen images while I was experiencing an event. Maybe I'm becoming more comfortable within the Ether. I don't know if I will experience this again, but it was quite an experience to have. I pulled the beige blanket back from her face, and I knew that I knew this person. Unfortunately, now I cannot remember who it was, but I definitely remember having known who she was. I remember seeing her face in full color and the texture of her facial features. Right after I had pulled the blanket off her face, her spirit body drifted out of the physical body, and she began talking to me. I do not now remember what she said, but we did have a conversation for several minutes. I know that part of it was about her family outside grieving for her. I went back to the family, and I told them not to worry about this person because she would be fine. She had given me several things to tell them and those things apparently made them feel better. I must have clicked out after this. However, I felt rather warm inside knowing that I had done some good for someone. It also felt like I had been in an area where an earthquake just happened and so many people had died. I was glad to be of service.

31

Eyes of an Angel

(5/6/2005)

I had been reading a new book that Paul Elder wrote called *Eyes of an Angel*. Paul is Skip's assistant for the Remote Viewing program at TMI. I met him at my RV class in November. When I took my Manifestation and Creation Squared class I stopped in at the Nancy Penn Center to say "Hi" to Skip, and Paul was also there. I was unaware that he would be there. Paul told me that he had just published a book. I did not know he was writing one. He said he had a copy in his room, and we went to his room; he signed it for me, and I paid him for it. Paul's book is about his experiences at TMI and beyond. I have been reading it and noticing similarities between his adventures and mine. But, today I came to a place where he had described something as follows:

"There was an abrupt spinning motion, and seconds later I found myself standing in front of an enormous building. It looked like something out of ancient Greece or Rome. Built of marble or granite, it must have been at least fifty feet high. Huge pillars spanned the front of the imposing structure and an immense stairway led up to a large arched entry." Does this sound familiar to any of you? "Throngs of people moved in and out of the build-ing. The beauty of the interior was breathtaking. Ornate pillars drew my eyes upwards to astonishing domed ceilings. Flawlessly painted in flowing murals, the intricate images were stunning. The paintings seemed to move and flow with a life of their own. I had never seen anything so exquisite!"

He went on to ask, "What is this place?" His guide answered, "This is our Library and Hall of Records." Then, he continued, "As we began to walk along a huge corridor, on either side were row after row of shelves filled with books and odd cylinders. It occurred to me that the cylinders might contain scrolls."

Well, if this is not exactly the place that I had been to many times myself, then I am not in a sane frame of mind! I was pro-foundly affected by his description of the Library and how tall and beautiful it is on the inside. Also, his description of the shelves and scrolls is just uncanny. I have not spoken to Paul about this. His descriptions of some things were much better than mine. However, this is a validation for me that what I have been experiencing on my own travels is REAL!

(5/7/2005)

While reading more of Paul's book about his description of the Library, I also found the following to be true: Paul goes on to describe a chair that his guide Meldor was sitting on and then it disappeared. Meldor says, "It was completely real to your percep-tion, was it not? You could have sat on it as I did. It was very real, but at the same time it was only a temporary construction of my mind; whereas the Library that you visited was much more permanent and substantial. It too, however, was created by thought. But it is reinforced by the conscious energy of billions of souls. Each and every visitor to the building maintains and perpetually reinforces the reality of the structure." To me this means that the Library would look essentially the same to anyone who visits it, and they would have a similar description of it. This, for me, again reinforces the realness of my visits and experiences to the Library. It is just sooo Cool isn't it?

32

Manifestation and Creation²

I just Love going to TMI. Each time I go there I am even more affected by the place and the people and the course activities. It is just such a pleasure to meet, talk to and become friends with such like-minded people. Too bad we don't live in the same place; it would be a lot easier to multiply our combined thoughts and powers.

The MC² class is a high-focused energy and empowering experience that leads you to a loving communion with the creative life force. During this class we learned how to manifest what you desire, and to bring this potentiality into our physical existence.

There were only 15 people in our class and the teacher, Joe, was a fantastic guy, and Macca, the other trainer, was a great teacher too. We had a blast the entire week.

We started out on Saturday by raising our energy levels to create some terrific effects later in the week. None of us could have enjoyed ourselves more. We even had a father and son team from Moose Jaw, Canada there. What a great gift to a teenager, to bring them to TMI and expose them to such fantastic things at such a young age. This class took place at Roberts Mountain

Retreat, where Bob Monroe had lived. This was my first experience there, and I highly recommend it to anyone who has the opportunity to attend a class there. It is set apart from the Nancy Penn Center and is a very spiritual place. They even have a swimming pool, but it was too cold to have it open. We were the first class up there for the season so they didn't have everything quite up to speed yet. We had a lot of classes in Bob Monroe's cabin, where he did a lot of his writing during his time there. You can feel his presence everywhere you go.

Our classes were not just about rolling the dice and bending spoons. Actually, our main activity was to do healings for the week. We did healings on each other in healing circles and distance healings for others as well. We had a local person come into our healing circle who is a TMI employee who had a tremendous amount of medical problems and we did a healing on him. We also did Earth healings, and long distance healing for others. We all found the healing aspects of the class very moving. The healing we did on each other was tremendous. I asked for healing on my nasal sinuses, since my sinuses had been terrible. Having a week at TMI without any nasal problems at all rewarded me. That was the first time my sinuses had been clear at TMI out of the three trips I made there.

We were able to light fluorescent light bulbs with our hands one night, and bending spoons was another terrific activity. I was fortunate enough to be very good at the bending of spoons category. I was the one to whom others came to get help in bending their spoons. In fact, I had to stop bending spoons and forks because I was doing it so much we were running out of them!

MANIFESTATION AND CREATION[2]

Joe apparently had been observing all of us during the week and towards the end of the week, he mentioned to me that he had a Vegas workshop coming up in June, and he recommended that I attend it too. He said that I have a lot of energy and that I'd be good for his Vegas class! I told him that I would go to Atlantic City this week to try out my newfound skills, and I would call him later to sign up for his Vegas class. This was pretty neat stuff. The class is much more than dice influencing or bending spoons. Whenever you go to TMI, you feel the connection to the whole place --the buildings, the people, the Crystals, and the grounds. By just walking the grounds you feel connected to the whole of life, the Earth and the Universe itself. It is truly a magical, mystical and spiritual place.

For myself I can honestly say that since my first class, the Gateway Voyage last September, my life has been completely transformed into something I never could have contemplated previously. I have met so many fabulous people and encountered so many new thoughts and ideas that it changed my entire belief system from one of believing to one of knowing. I have been placed on a path I could not have dreamed possible previous to my going to TMI. My entire world has been transformed into one of beauty, knowing, and believing that anything is possible in this lifetime. I have been truly blessed; not only by TMI, but also by all of the people I met there. I thank each of you for being a part of my journey through this lifetime. I have found along the way that I have known many of you in past lives. That in itself is a truly wondrous gift, and one that I will always cherish.

33

Dee

(5/8/2005)

The things that happen in the Astral you have to experience for yourself, and you are the only one who can feel if they are real or not. Therefore, I fully expect at times that you think that I have made this stuff up. However, I will tell you they did happen to me, and I know it was all-real.

I told you that in my travels a woman from my church, who was a medium, had shown up a couple of times. Well, she asked me when this first happened, if I knew anything about her that I wanted to share with her. At the time, I had to say, "No," which was the truth. I had met her a couple of times in the Ether, and she either tagged along or she took me to a couple of places. We had gone to the Healing Temple a couple of times but nothing out of the ordinary had happened, except that we had both clicked out. When that happens, you are usually experiencing something in the Ether that your mind cannot comprehend, or something that you are not supposed to remember until some future time. This has happened a couple of times, but I did not think much of it because it does happen a lot when you travel in the Ether.

TALKING WITH ANGELS

One day Denise said to me that she had to talk to me about those adventures. Dee had been traveling in the Astral and talking to Angels (she called them Angels, I called them helpers -- but no matter) all of her life. She explained to me that she had begun to feel sexually aroused when these adventures were happening. She has a friend who is also very active in the Astral and asked her if something happening in the Astral can affect your body in the Physical. Her friend told her absolutely! She also told Dee that when Dee was at the Healing Temple with me that we were probably having astral sexual experiences, and that was why she was feeling sexually aroused in the physical. Dee said that when we went to the temple, or if we met by the willow tree, we were having these sexual experiences, which was fine with me, but I did not remember any of these things happening at the time. Dee told me that she was experiencing her sexuality being reawakened by these occurrences. She was very surprised that this was happening to her, especially since this was not something that she had been looking to do. I had to ask her, if she was out there initially looking to meet up with me or did this original meeting just happen since I had been sending her some of my travels. Dee said that originally we had met by accident as she was not out there looking for me or deliberately coming into my travels. She had no idea when I was doing them or what I was doing in them until after I had done them. That is, until she started to show up. Again, she can astral travel at will, so for her to find me out there is not a big deal for her. But after she had realized that when we were meeting we were having these sexual experiences in the astral, she figured that she had to confront me to see if I was consciously doing this to her. During these times Dee was experiencing these sexual happenings in the Physical. If I was doing this she wanted to know. At the time I had to say that I was not consciously doing this. But by this time, if I am remembering my time frames correctly, I started remembering these meetings happening. I was remembering having these astral encounters with her! I have learned that these astral sexual encounters are not uncommon with people who visit the astral. These sexual encounters are something that cannot be described in words. They are literally beyond description. I cannot describe the blissful, exciting, unbelievable feelings that take place in the astral when this happens. Too bad we can't experience it in the physical, or can we?

Now that I was aware of what was happening in the astral between us, I was somewhat taken aback, because I had known Dee for two years or more and there was never an attraction between us in the physical. Again, I had not been astral traveling very long, so all of this stuff was brand new to me. Dee told me that she had never experienced anything like these sexual encounters before in the astral, and that something from the astral had never affected her in the physical. Apparently we were in uncharted territory.

Anyway, we now had a connection. These astral meetings were becoming more frequent and very nice. It seemed that whenever I went out there I found her at the willow tree and I never got any further because we just stayed there and made love. It was really neat. But, one day, I got very sexually aroused, and I was just sitting at my computer not traveling anywhere. I could not believe that this was happening. So, I told myself that it wasn't happening. I e-mailed Dee and told her what had happened, and at what time it happened, and asked her if she was with me in the astral at that time. She told me that at that time she was in the Ether and that we were together! She said, "It's about time that you felt what I have been going through for a few weeks." I could not believe that this was happening. However, I definitely knew that something was going on.

So now, what do I do? We do have this soul connection, and it is very real. I cannot describe to you how powerful it is. We have been soul mates, but I did not know where or when we had been together before. We decided to get together in the physical and see where it would take us.

One night as we were winding down, we decided to have one more round and what a round it was. As we were getting into the thick of things, we were suddenly experiencing an astral experience at the same time. Dee confirmed this. Spirit really is something. We actually experienced making love on the astral plane at the same time as we were in the physical. All I can say is that we both experienced the same thing. Both our physical bodies were shaking like no tomorrow, and when we were finished, we were both physically drained and could not move for about half an hour. We were just totally wasted. No drugs were needed here, believe me. I wish that there was a way for me to describe it to you, but I just cannot think of one. Words cannot describe the feeling.

Since that time we have experienced another quite extraordinary event. Because we were able to experience the astral in the physical, I asked spirit if it would be possible for us to achieve a merging of our souls in the physical. The answer to my question occurred one night while we were just holding each other. I started to caress Dee on the back when all of a sudden I felt my hand going *through* her body and bringing her into me. I asked, "Did you feel the same sensation?" She said, "Yes." Then, our souls *merged* together in our physical bodies. This was the most exquisite thing that either of us could ever have imagined. Neither of us had ever heard of this type of thing happening to anyone, ever. We both felt extremely blessed that this had occurred to us at the same time!

When I went to MC² at TMI someone asked me a question about Denise and I. So I related the above story to them. Then Macca, one of the teachers in the course, asked if we could reproduce the soul connection in the physical that we had experienced once before. I said that we had not tried to reproduce the experience, as it was such an impossible experience the first time that the thought hadn't even crossed our minds about trying to make it happen again. But, I decided to ask the Angels if Dee and I could experience that soulful experience again. Be careful what you ask spirit for because you may get the answer, in spades.

What we found was that one evening, after spending some time together, we were suddenly overcome with this soul merging feeling again just by pure accident. It was a blissful feeling that I hope each and every one of you can experience some time in your lifetime. Then, later on that night, Dee placed her hand on my heart, just for the act of caressing me, and all of a sudden I felt this merging beginning again. It was just incredible, believe me, and totally unexpected. We both felt the same feelings of bliss and the merging of our souls again. This just about blew us both away. It may have been due to the fact that I had just returned from TMI and my heart Chakra was wide open. I don't know. You also have to remember that Dee is very spiritual, and she can come and go and talk to the Angels anytime and anywhere. The same event occurred two more times on that evening. We were both just totally wiped out by this occurrence and fell into a deep sleep afterwards.

The next morning we both woke up. As we were recounting the events of the previous evening, and I was caressing her, I suddenly felt my hand entering her body. The other times it was basically from Dee's side that this occurred, and I did not think anything of it since she is the more spiritually attuned person of the two of us, so I just figured that she had the power to do these things herself. But when this happened to me, I just could not believe it. And, again we experienced our souls merging here in the physical world.

I have to answer Macca's question about weather I could reproduce this soul merging in the physical world on demand. After thinking about it, I would have to say that "Yes, it is reproducible", at least in our case. I wish you could experience this just once in your lifetime. You would be a different, more tolerant and spiritual person than you could ever have thought possible because it would change your total perspective about this life and the next.

On a different note; one day I mentioned to Dee that Rick had brought his son to a TMI class and that they were from a place called Moose Jaw in Canada. Dee said to me," His name is not Bub Hill, is it?" I replied, "No, but there is a channeler that Rick gets together with, and he gave me a CD from that person." Sure enough, I looked at the name on the CD, and it was by Bub Hill! Dee had been in touch with him for a long time on the Internet, and they corresponded frequently. What do you figure the odds of that happening? Pretty long I'd say !

NOTE:

This concludes Part One. I will forever be in the debt of The Monroe Institute and their magnificent teachers for starting me on my spiritual journey. My kudos to all of you guys.

Part Two

34

Are They Listening?

(4/30/2005)

Denise and I had a merging of our souls, but I was not prepared for what happened directly afterward. The Angels took advantage of that opportunity, which is not unusual for them to do, and took me away for an adjustment as soon as we got back from our own spiritual journey. We were both unprepared for this, but were not shaken by it since it had happened many times before. I just do not know when they will finish these adjustments. When I asked, they said that I needed them because I had to catch up to Dee, and I had started from a place far behind her. This particular adjustment had a real time effect on me though. In the past I had noticed an easier time communicating with and receiving contact from the Angels. But after this session, which was intense, but not as intense as some others I had experienced, I was told that since I had started from a higher vibrational level that they were able to adjust me easier and get more in, in the time allowed for the session. I immediately knew what would happen in the future anytime Dee and I merged -- they would come and take me away. They take advantage of things like that.

TALKING WITH ANGELS

What Dee immediately noticed after I was through with this adjustment was that while holding her and placing my hands on her shoulders, I now had healing power in my hands. She said she could feel the warmth of my hands going into her body. I checked my hands, but they were cool to the touch, not warm, as she had described. I placed them back onto her shoulders, and she said that she could definitely feel the healing power of my hands. I said, "It's about time that I see some tangible results from all of the adjustments that I have been through." Dee cracked, "Don't get cocky" which is a statement I have often used myself on my son who would often do well in a subject at school then slack off and not do as well on the next test. When we do well at something we all have a tendency to back off and let it slide. But, in this case I was not being "cocky". I was just stating that at last I have some tangible evidence for myself that whatever the Angels are doing to me during these adjustments, I can finally see some results. I think Dee understood what I meant, but I did get a déjà vu moment there when she told me not to get cocky.

I was not sure that the healing ability that I suddenly had would stick around. I thought that maybe, since there had just been an adjustment to me, that it would fade and dissipate in a short period. I have tried to use my healing hands on Dee since then, and she has told me, "Yes you still have healing hands." Dee is a Reiki Master, so she knows about the healing power of touching a person with your hands and what can be accomplished. She said, "Do you want to be a Reiki healer? I could teach you." I told her, "Thank you for the offer, but I am not really into the healing aspects of spirituality, although I do think that it is very valuable." I told her I would be happy if I could just heal her, since she has a disabling syndrome that is very painful. In fact, she is in pain all the time. I told her that if I could just heal her, I would be content. Therefore, I work on her daily now, and we have to see how we do down the road. I am so grateful to the Angels for using me in this manner because I had never even thought about it until it actually happened. I guess those guys know what is best.

Ever since I turned myself over to God last year, my life has not been the same. I told God that I would take the passenger seat of the car and allow Him to drive wherever He wanted me to go, that I was just along for the ride. Since I have done that, my life has completely changed... for the better.

Since being able to "merge on demand" so to speak, another event has begun to transpire. My body has been adjusted from time to time with vibrations from the Angels. Well, since Dee and I have discovered this merging process, the Angels found a new way to come and get me to make these adjustments, and they are not concerned about when it occurs. Sometimes I can recognize when the Angels are talking to me now, so I try to be more open and listen. I was told by them that when Dee and I do this merging process, it raises my energy level to a point at which they can jump in and start to do an adjustment to me at will. They have no sense of linear time like we do, so they just come right in and take over as soon as my energy level is sufficient for them to make these adjustments to me. They say it is easier for them to adjust me since they are starting from a higher energy level to begin with. This has become somewhat of a battle between them and us, because now the Angels just jump in anytime to take me away with them without any consideration of what is happening to me in the physical world. Since Dee can talk to them anytime, she has scolded them for jumping in at inappropriate times and has asked them to stop many times when they have jumped in. Sometimes they listen, but other times they either ignore her request or tell her that they have to continue with the adjustment at their time for some reason. However, they never explain the reason.

(5/5/2005)

Dee and I had another merging of our souls session, and before we did, I told her that the Angels would be back right afterwards, so that she should be ready for the adjustment. We did the merging of our souls and sure enough, immediately after we were finished, they came and started in on me. This particular adjustment was very intense this time; I hope it accomplished some real changes in me, although they do not tell you these kinds of things even when you ask them. Dee said that she was told by one of my Angels that the session would be a short one. Yeah right! Angels do not have any sense of linear time. I don't know how long or short the session was, but Dee said it was not short in duration. But, it was intense in its effect on my body; my entire body was in spasm at different times. Now, I am used to these adjustments so I pretty much know what to expect, but this time it was definitely more intense than others in the past. I am fully aware of my surroundings whenever these occur, but I do not have any control over the reactions of my physical body.

ARE THEY LISTENING?

My entire being was being affected, so much so that after a while Dee had to tell them, "That's enough for now, stop!" When I heard Dee say this I knew that they should stop because Dee is attuned to what I can withstand. When she told them to stop, I also asked them to stop. They are generally agreeable to this, and they did stop for a brief period. I am usually wiped out for a while after these types of adjustments, but this time I was really sweating profusely afterwards. I needed a towel to dry myself off. This was unusual. I knew that Dee was correct when she had told them it was enough.

We have learned that the Angels like to come to me when I am at the higher vibrational levels. Thus, we will be prepared the next time we merge for an intense session with them right after we are back from merging. They always come immediately afterwards, they don't even give me a chance to breathe. In fact, one time they told me to hurry up so that they could start on me! At least they did have the courtesy to wait until we were finished. Maybe I should get them a clock so that I can tell them to give me five minutes before they start!

35

Michael

I have been experiencing some extraordinary events in my life recently and they continue to happen at a rate that astounds even me! I had several vibrational changes done to me by the Angels in the last couple of months, and they had some terrific changes in my life. I am more open to everyone and to everything around me. My heart Chakra is wide open and great things occur. These vibrational changes now occur at an even greater frequency than they had before. I know when they are going to happen to me, and I know how many in the series there will be. I am able to perceive more from the Angels when they want me to know something. I still have a hard time communicating directly to them, but on occasion I now have a conversation with my guides or Angels and that is a terrific thing to be able to do. Some of you are probably able to do this all the time, like Denise, but this was new territory for me.

The other night, I was awakened by the Angels for another adjustment. I was very shaken by this adjustment, and I was told that this had to be done and completed at that time. In the past when one of these adjustments took a long time and was draining on me physically, I would ask them to stop and continue at a later time. This time it was different. They said, "No, it has to be done now." Then the most incredible thing happened. I realized that this adjustment was done to me by Michael, not just any Michael, but Michael the Archangel!

That just blew me away, because I never even thought about something like that happening, especially to me! I received attention from Michael the Archangel, which was just incomprehensible to me. Why would he be interested in me? Well, I found out that Michael, as well as any of the other Archangels, are interested in all of us. I was told that this is not really an uncommon happening, that they do these kinds of things all of the time.

I had been made aware of these kinds of things over the past several months but never did I dream that something like this would occur. However, I was told we are all deserving of this type of attention, and we can all experience this type of attention if we open ourselves up to it. I am continually amazed at all of the things that are happening. I try to share them, but some happen so quickly that I cannot comprehend nor remember all of them to completely relate them to you.

The most incredible part of this adjustment was that sometime during the event Archangel Michael literally swooped his hand down into my body, directly into my Heart Chakra! I actually felt his presence inside my body. I will understand if you think that I was dreaming, but I can only wish that you could experience it. I know that this happened to me! I felt him reach down and touch me inside my body. I cannot explain the feeling but it was real. After that happened, I just broke down and cried for about half an hour because it was so incredible. The hardest part for me to comprehend was how was I worthy enough for such an event to have occurred? I was told that each and every one of us is worthy and that it does occur with relative frequency to people on this Earth.

I do not know why the Angels have adjusted me, but I do know that they are supposed to bring me up to a higher level in the spiritual realm. I also do not know what to expect when I am at these higher frequency levels, although I had been told by Dee that I now have healing power in my hands. This is not something that I have been trained to do, nor is it something that I intended to do; it is just something that has happened to me since my vibrational levels have been upgraded.

I hope that I can do some good with it. In fact, I am using this newfound ability to do as much good for others as possible, because healing someone is one of the greatest gifts that we can offer to them in this physical world. So, for as long as it lasts, I will help as many people as possible and do whatever good that I can do.

Last night, I was awakened in the middle of the night for another of those adjustments. It lasted for about ten to fifteen minutes and when it was over the Angels were kind enough to me to let me fall gently back to sleep. I guess they knew I had to go to work, so they let me get some needed rest. After some of these adjustments my body is not ready for anything; sometimes I get very agitated and sometimes the vibrational level is so high that it takes a long time for my body to calm down. I do not know when this will happen to me again, but judging from the past few weeks I can expect more adjustments in the near future. I have been able to contact Michael since his entrance into my life, and I have found him to be very approachable and very nice too. I was just so awestruck by the fact that he would take an interest in me, but after talking to him for a while I can see that he is just a part of the whole picture. I am getting some small glimpses on occasion of the bigger reason for these things happening to me, but I have not been able to put the mosaic together at this point.

36

Metatron

(5/7/2005)

Last night was a wild ride for me. I was up most of the night. My Angels were preparing me for something, but what that something was, I did not know. All night they kept after me and after me, adjusting me, sometimes very heavily and for some long time periods. Dee did not know what was happening. She continued to consult them, but all they said was that it needed to be done and it could not be put off. Somewhere along the timeframe Dee heard some mention of Metatron, but she did not know what that meant because he did not contact her directly. But this morning, when what turned out to be the last adjustment for the night (a very intense adjustment that shook me to the core), we found out what the whole evening was about. Right at the end of the final adjustment for the night, I felt the hand of an Archangel delve into my body again, as Michael had done previously. But the feeling was different; it was not Michael who did this. I told Dee that someone touched me but it was not Michael. Then she knew who it was. She automatically said it was Archangel Metatron. She said that was why his name came to her and that was the reason for the whole night of adjustments. It was to ready my body for Archangel Metatron to touch me inside. Metatron is the highest of the Archangels.

Now that it had been done, my body was in need of some time off, so I was treated to a few minutes of rest before I had to start my day. This was a different experience for me, a session happening through the entire night. Dee and I both keep wondering when my body will be fully adjusted to whatever vibrational level they want me to be at, but we never got an answer to that question. I suppose they know best. But, just small tremors instead of the whole body spasm types of adjustments that I am currently having would be nice for a change. I will have to wait and see what happens the next time they come to take me for a session. At least I still have healing hands, which is important to me, so I can continue to help Dee as much as possible

37

Merging

(5/9/2005)

This morning, while sitting holding each other on the couch,
Dee and I had this deep desire to merge again. We had both been
resisting this for a while because whenever we do that, the Angels
come and take me away for an adjustment, and those had been
getting more and more numerous as the days wore on. Dee had
asked them how long this would continue, and she was told that
it would continue for several more weeks until I reach the peak.
It was very cryptic but that is all she could get about it. Hopefully
at that point, if the adjustments continue they will be less intense
and more manageable than they are now.

I was told to go ahead and merge, let Dee make her phone
call to mom, and then they will take me for an adjustment. I
asked, "Will it be a long or short one and will it be intense?" As
usual they did not give me an answer. I guess they really have no
conception of the depth of these adjustments or the timeframe
of how long they are since they are in the spirit world. So Dee
and I merged, although before I even told her what the Angels
had imparted to me, she said that she was already merging with

me prior to my telling her what they had said. It was a totally blissful and incredible time. Then she called her mom, which she does every morning and evening. Again as usual, the second she finished her phone call, they came and took me away. Dee said, "You'd think they could wait a minute", but that is not the way they work. I had another adjustment for about fifteen minutes and they departed. I don't know when they are coming back, but I do feel them when they are coming, so does Dee. We can usually tell when they are around. Sometimes we shoo them away, which works occasionally, but most of the time we can only push them off for a few minutes before they come in on their own and do what they have to do. They make no apologies for their actions, they just state, "This has to be done so that I can catch up to Denise." Why I have to catch up to her we do not know. We do know that there must be a reason for it, so we pretty much let them do their thing for the time being. We also recognize that judging from all of the experiences that we had been through during the last couple of months, whatever they have in store must be truly dramatic. We are open to it, and we are waiting for some new type of experience, one that, if it is anything like our past ones, will be truly mind-boggling to be sure.

(5/10/2005)

Dee said that they were getting me ready for a visit from Yeshuah, and that is what all of the tuning was for. The Angels told me that now my physical body was in a high enough vibrational state that they could come and get me at any time. Of course, the

MERGING

first chance they got they did just that. We were not feeling well so we decided just to lie in bed and take it easy. Wouldn't you know it, as soon as we decided to do that they came, swooped in and took me for a short tuning up trip. They promised Dee it would be short, and thankfully it was, because I was not really feeling well and was not in the mood for the adjustment at that time. I told them to come back when I was feeling better. I had to admit that I was beginning to tire of these adjustments. Naturally, they said they would continue for several more weeks, so I just had to grin and bear it.

(5/20/2005)

Since the encounter with Archangel Metatron Dee told me that I would experience another person visiting me, one she calls Yeshuah. She did not know when He would come, only that He would come to me soon. Well, a couple of days went by and then after another night when I was treated to several severe adjustments in a short time frame, Dee asked the Angel Megga, one of our angels, why these were coming so fast and furious. She was told that he had to do them now. She even asked him to stop for a while because she was beginning to get concerned about my welfare with these very severe adjustments, but Megga told her that he could not stop them. Later, during the night after one particularly intense but short adjustment, I was told that something special was going to happen later. I was not told what it would be but that it would be special. After that the adjustments had stopped, except for some rather mild adjustments that did not disturb my sleep. When I awoke in the morning, Dee said to me that the Angels told her that Yeshuah had visited me during the night. I said that I thought that would happen but I did not recall any visitation by Him or anyone else that evening. I did not doubt that it happened, as we do not recall many things that occur during our sleep. It's just that I would have liked to remember that encounter and to have asked Him some questions too.

It started to happen that whenever Dee would just touch me in almost any manner, the Angels would jump at the occasion to take me for another adjustment. This got to be a bit of a pain because it would happen at anytime. If Dee just touched me in a caring way, they would come and get me. Again, I was told that my vibrational level was a bit higher now, and they could bring me along faster by doing this. Of course, I was beginning to tire of that fact, and I really had very little control over it although no adjustments ever happened when I was driving or working. At least they had the consideration to do all of the adjustments when I was at home with Dee. Dee was getting upset also because she literally could not touch me anymore without my being taken away by them for a while.

This went on for another week. Then, after one more adjustment, I was told that I was now at a high enough vibrational level that having Dee touch me would not be a problem anymore. They said that they could still take me anytime they wished, but they would now be a little more concerned with their timing. This turned out to be true. But, their idea of timing is not what we would consider good timing. You have to remember that we are dealing with non-physical entities here who do not relate to time. When they say, "We'll be back later", it could actually be five minutes later, which it was many times.

Dee was set to take a trip to see her son in Florida so the Angels figured that they would have to get in their adjustments quickly. For the few days before she left I had many, many adjustments. In fact, the night before she was to leave, they were at it most of the night. Not only did they continually come for me but the adjustments were some of the most intense that I had ever experienced. Dee was concerned so she asked Megga to take it easy on me. She was surprised when a new Angel appeared; she said her name was Macedonia and that she would be my Angel from then on. Dee was told that it was important for me to catch up to her as soon as possible and this was an integral part of that process. Without even asking, or considering what either one of us could or would say about this, it was done.

38

Obsidian Tears

The other night while Dee and I were sleeping, the Angels decided to come for another adjustment. While being adjusted I began to feel an urgency to merge with Dee during it. I told her this, and she said that she had been feeling the same urgency but did not want to interfere if not asked by me. I told her that the Angels were urging this so it was okay. She placed her hand over my heart as she usually does to merge and off we went. As usual, I always start out with a quickening of my breath and shortly after that I am hit with this overwhelming feeling of helplessness, due to the fact that I begin to feel Dee's pain from her Reflexive Sympathetic Dystrophy Syndrome (RSDS), and I usually begin to weep for a couple of minutes. This was not distressing to me because it happens each and every time that Dee and I merge. It is part of the merging process as we literally delve into each other's bodies. After this short time I regained my composure, and I was ready for whatever happened from there on. I never know exactly what will happen, especially when the Angels are involved in the process.

This adventure turned out to be related to one of my past life experiences from a week or so earlier. I had been aware of the fact that I was at one time a Native American Indian from the 1800's. There may have been more than one lifetime involved, but I had not put together that kind of information at the time. I remembered reading an American Indian e-card from a website, and I felt a terrific connection with it, especially since it had to do with Obsidian rocks that I had found to be impossible to even hold. I found this out one day before Dee and I had gotten together. It was actually the first time that we had gone anywhere together. It was to a rock and mineral show, where Dee had to pick up some stones for her jewelry making and for the church store, which also sells stones. While we were looking at the different types of stones, of which I know virtually nothing, Dee explained the different stones and what their uses were to me. I picked up these shiny black stones, which turned out to be Obsidian stones. Obsidian stones are volcanic black glass that when held up to the light are translucent. They are commonly called Apache tears. A legend says that they were once tears shed by the wives of a band of Apache warriors who were killed by the U.S. military in retaliation for their raid on an Arizona settlement. I had to drop them out of my hands immediately since I literally could not hold these stones. I never felt anything like this in my life! They were like fire to me when I held them. I tried again, and the same thing happened, I could not hold them in my hands even for a second, the feeling was too intense. Dee told me that the Obsidian stones were a Native American stone and that they were very powerful because they have metaphysical properties. You usually put a couple of them in your pocket to keep your body in balance. I could not see why I had such an adverse reaction to these stones; I had never before seen them in my life.

After reading the Indian e-card and feeling such an overwhelming dread, I came to the conclusion that I was involved with this story. I had been an Indian involved with the Trail of Tears and in the catastrophe that had occurred. I found myself back in time as an Indian being driven from the reservation by soldiers, and my family being killed in the process. I had been weeping and was full of rage. I even remembered attacking the white soldiers in revenge for what they had done to my family. During my attack on them I had been killed. I was then shown two other more recent times when I had been killed in battle during World War I and World War II.

I was being shown these connections with my past lives because they were all related. They all had to do with my experiencing the loss of others around me when I had no control over the situation. It hit me like a ton of bricks when I realized that I had been experiencing these things because of their relationship to my present lifetime. In my present lifetime I always had a feeling of unworthiness that had kept me from grabbing the brass ring when it was presented to me. This had happened many times. I would always go only so high in any of my businesses or working environments, and when it was possible to take the next step (which would have been to get over the hurdles and really start to make great strides), I would always fall back, not by conscious choice but by what I realized were my feelings of unworthiness. I was not worthy of being able to have the good life in this lifetime. I always fell short in those aspirations. It had been something that I had been aware of but never knowing the reason why I could not attain it. I had done this many times in my present life, and I had thwarted myself each and every time. Now, at last I had figured out why this was happening to me.

However, being shown where it had started, and being aware of the fact that this feeling is truly unwarranted; but I was never in control of the situation where people around me were killed by others through no fault of my own. This realization had a powerful effect on me in that I could now see where this feeling came from, why it happened, how it happened, and realizing that it was beyond my control, that I could now forgive myself and release myself from these feelings of guilt that I had clung to throughout so many lifetimes. This was very cathartic for me and something that truly changed my life. I cannot explain what a spiritual and uplifting feeling went through me! I had come through the desert and come out the other side, and I was set free by this realization. I could now allow myself the ability to experience success in this lifetime as I had never experienced it before. During my regression on this subject, I asked the question, "Why was this reoccurring?" I was told by my Angels this was the place and the time for this to happen. In other words, I was doing exactly what I was supposed to be doing at this time.

After reading the poem about the Apache Indians I felt a chilling effect upon my body, and I knew that I had been a part of that type of massacre. When I read about the Obsidian stones, I knew that I was familiar with them. This was my starting point. I had been rendered incapable of fighting back at that time and my life had to end along with others. We had no choice and that became my own nemesis in lives during the past hundred and fifty or so years. While looking at the events in many past lives and coming to the realization that these situations were beyond my control when they happened, it allowed me to shed my feelings of guilt of not having done the best job that I could do under the circumstances and allowed me to lift this burden from my shoulders. Finally, I could get on with my life and succeed.

I knew that I was in a place of in-between at this time. I had been trying to start moving on with my life, but the timing was not right. I was seemingly stuck exactly where I was. You see, during my hiatus from the work-a-day world, I had been developing my relationship with Dee. That was something we both needed to do, and we were enjoying each and every day. During this time, the Angels also had ideas for me. The adjustments were being done on an almost daily basis for a couple of months straight. I do not know when these periods of adjustment will end, but I do know that I have been raised up from a low vibrational level to one where I can now feel the Angels most of the time when they want to communicate with me.

It is very interesting that immediately after the above-mentioned experiences those things suddenly began to move in a forward direction. Coincidence? I think not.

Having completed this I now set out on a new path. Again, I had to put God in charge. He takes me where He wants me to be, and I just do whatever He tells me to do. When I got to this point of my journey I found that the road ahead had been unblocked for me. I told the Angels that I understood the reason that I had not been doing additional work up to this point. I also knew that Dee and I had been allowed to have this time together because we both deserved it.

39

Light Being

(6/18/2005)

Dee still has feelings in her legs and feet and the circulation is continuing. The other day her doctor was very pleased her circulation and feeling were returning. Of course, when she said the Angels did it, he gave the obligatory whatever works response, although not really believing it. It would be too much for an MD to handle if we explained the whole process to him, so we are just enjoying the benefits of the Angels work.

This morning I had an interesting experience with the Angels. I was lying down and all of a sudden an Indian showed up. He was standing in full regalia, and he had a large stick in one hand adorned with feathers and ribbons. He was just standing there with a neutral look on his face. I mentioned this to Dee, and she said, "Ask him if he is Running Bull." I did, and it took a while for him to communicate the answer to me, possibly because this was our first communication. He finally did get his message across to me, that he was Running Bull and then he broke out into a broad smile. Dee said that he has been with her since birth. While he was standing there a Light Being came into view. This again was a new experience for me as I do not as a rule communicate with these Spirit Entities on my own. I said to Dee, "A Light Being just showed up" and she asked, "Who is it?" I said that I did not know. The entity was a female, and she said her name was "Ooohh" something or other. I could not make it out. So I left it at that for the moment. Shortly after that the Angel Madagascar came into view. This was the first time that I could actually see Madagascar, even though I have communicated with her several times before, and Dee has seen her and spoken to her many times. She is very beautiful with long black hair and a beautiful smile on her face --glowing actually. She said that we were making excellent progress, and we were to continue exactly as we have been. She told me that we were exactly on schedule and that everything would be fine in the long run. She also said that she would help me with my shoulder pain and my sinuses. I told Dee this, and she said that was the answer to her question to Madagascar. She had inquired about the Angel helping me along with helping her.

I focused on the Light Being again, and she said that her name was Oohnashrah and she was the "scheduler". It was her job to make sure everything happened when it was supposed to happen. She told me that we were right on schedule, and we did not have to worry about anything. Things were all taken care of, and they will happen exactly when they were supposed to happen. I said, "Thank you for the update." Immediately after this, an Angel walked in with a bathrobe and slippers on. He sat down on the couch, put his feet up on the futon and sat back to eat his Twizzlers. He did not say anything; he was just enjoying the Twizzlers. Then, Archangel Michael appeared and told me that we were doing just fine and not to worry about any financial matters, that they would be taken care of soon. I have been told by the Angels that it will all be okay, but I am still going along from month to month trying to makes ends meet. So far I have been successful, although I come very close to not being able to make some payment or another regularly. I just wish they would hurry up on that part of things. I think I have been without for long enough.

Soon after they departed. This was the first time that I had a conversation with many Angels and a spirit at one time.

40

Yeshuah

(6/19/2005)

When I sat down in church this morning a feeling came over me that gave me the chills. I immediately sensed that something was going to happen at services. After the opening prayer I stayed seated and did not immediately go up front for spiritual healing. As I sat there my mind wandered, and I wondered what was supposed to happen. When nothing seemed to be happening, I decided to go up for spiritual healing, which is a laying on of hands by another person to heal whatever needs healing. When I went up and sat in front of a healer, I told spirit to take me where it was that I was supposed to go. Immediately I saw myself diving into a large tropical lagoon that had a waterfall flowing into it. This waterfall was not high, maybe fifteen feet or so, and gently entered the lagoon. As I drank in the feeling of the cooling water and the surroundings, I looked around to see if I was by myself in the water, and I was. I scanned the shoreline to see if anyone was there and there was. Lo and behold I saw Jesus Christ waiting to greet me!

The last time I had seen Christ was when I went looking for

Him during a visit to the Library. I had gone to where He was preaching to a throng of people and, being about fifty yards off to His right hand side, I acknowledged Him, indicating that I was there to visit. He, on the other hand apparently knew that this was not the proper time for me to meet Him, so in a very casual way, He raised a finger on His one hand indicating a "No" to me by waving His finger in my direction. I immediately understood that this was not the time for the two of us to meet. So with that, I went off on another adventure and figured that we would meet whenever the timing was right.

When I swam over to where He was, I stood up from the water, and I immediately felt like I was dry. I did not need a towel or anything to dry myself. I did not look to see if I was wearing a bathing suit or clothing, which was irrelevant to the event unfolding at this time. As I stood up from the water I said, "Hello", and He acknowledged to me this was the time for us to meet. Apparently, He was referring to the last time we had seen each other when He was involved in a teaching situation for other people.

I was very excited to meet Him, and I told Him so. He acknowledged this fact and said, "We have met on many other occasions." I did not remember them but concluded that it must have been my spirit self that met with Him on these other occasions. I asked Him, "Why are we here today?" He indicated to me that He was here to answer some questions that I was wondering about lately. I acknowledged there were several questions that I had been wondering about, and that I was not able to get any definitive answers. He said, "Go ahead and ask what you need to know, and I will help you."

I asked my first question, which was about Denise, and the painful disease that she has. I told Him that the Angels were helping us out with her situation, through me, while we were getting a lot of these shifts occurring on a daily basis. He said, "Yes, the shifts were for Denise, and I should expect them to continue for quite a while." They had been occurring three or more times daily for the past few weeks, and we had noticed an improvement in her body as far as feelings and sensations go and the warming up of her feet and legs. I said, "Thank you for the help in this area, but I wanted to know if she would eventually be all right." He said, "Yes, she will." I told Him that I will continue to work with the Angels for as long as it takes, and Jesus said, "I know". Then He said, "Through this process you will also be helped with your physical problems" I thanked Him for that, although I had thought about asking more about those problems. He answered me before I could even think of the question. He acknowledged that Denise and I were doing extremely well, and that we were exactly where we were supposed to be at this point in time. This had been coming up a lot lately between the Angels and myself so I acknowledged that point.

I next asked Jesus, "How are my two children doing, and would they make their own way in the future?" He told me not to worry about either of them, that they would both be fine. This made feel a little calmer. Having Him say the children would be all right in the future really put my mind at ease. It was one less thing to trouble myself about.

Then Jesus asked me if I had any other matters to discuss

with Him. I said, "Just one other point." I was a bit leery of asking this especially to Him, but I figured that if He didn't know then no one would, so I went ahead and asked. I told Him that the only other real problem that I had at the present time was a lack of money to keep myself going. I told Him that I knew down the road I know I will be okay, but at the present time, I am short of capital and was wondering when this situation would change for me. He said, "Soon". I was continuing my search for some type of employment that suits my needs; I will continue to pursue it until something works out. With that as my answer, and coming from Him, I decided that the time was approaching for my needs to be fulfilled. I just have to have faith. I thanked Him for His answers to my several questions and bid Him farewell. He told me that we would meet again and I returned to my physical reality.

I was very moved by this experience, especially since it just came to me and was totally unexpected. I am deeply grateful to Jesus for coming to me and helping me out in my time of need. I do not know if I will meet Him again in this lifetime, but I am just very grateful to have had this opportunity.

41

Past Lives with Dee

(6/30/2005)

The Angels were doing a remarkable job with Dee. She was having many fewer leg spasms, and she was now able to feel her feet while walking. This was a tremendous advancement for her, one for which we were both very grateful. Except for the fact that the Angels just jump in any time they feel like it on me, the sessions with them were most intense and had gone from a purely physical muscle type of adjustment to one of mainly toning. They said that Dee had to participate in the toning also, and she did. The additional toning on her part increased the effects of the overall process. During the sessions, she felt different parts of her body being worked upon and afterward noticed definite changes in those areas. This will not be a short-term project, it is one which will take some time, but as long as it is helping, neither of us had any problems with the process. I have been told that this process will take many months of these types of sessions. I appreciate all of the love and help the Angels are sending to us during these times.

Today, after the angels finished with us, we decided to try to merge since we had the time and figured that they would leave us alone for a while since they had done much work on us already. We merged, and during this time I went to several past lives with Dee that we had experienced together without my directing the flow from one place to another. I had the intention of going to an American Indian experience with Dee, but beyond that I was taken by spirit to wherever they wanted me to go. I landed in an Indian tribe, which I felt was in the early 1800's in the West. In this life I was the mother and Dee was the father. Our child in that life was Dee's current son in this life. It always is fascinating to me to see who shows up in other lives that we have lived with and in what capacity they appear. There did not seem to be a lot of important information from this life beyond the fact of who was there, so I was quickly moved on to another life where I had interaction with Dee.

What I next saw was not your typical quiet or reserved life like the previous one with the Indian family. There I was running through the jungle, trying to get away from people from another tribe who were trying to track me down. This was in South America during the Aztec time frame; exactly what dates I do not know. Ultimately this tribe of people captured me. During this timeframe, the Aztecs, as well as many other tribes, believed in human sacrifice. After my capture and subsequent detention in their village, I was to be given up for human sacrifice. I did not recognize any people that I knew, although I was only there for a short period of time. But, the next thing I knew I was tied down on a sacrificial alter and was going to have my heart removed by the high priest. The high priest had on this gargoyle style of mask that was frightening. I knew that I was going to be sacrificed, and no amount of my pleading or trying to get away would change that. I was scared to death about what was going to happen to me. The priest took off his mask and looked right into my eyes. The high priest was none other than Denise! He looked at me with a knowing acknowledgement of what he was about to do, but it had to be done, and he just went about his business. The next part of this I remember as not actually happening to me physically but rather as an observer. I stood and watched as the priest cut open my body, removed my heart and held it up to the people while it was still beating. There was a great roar from the crowd at this, but thankfully I was quickly removed from that lifetime and sent to another where the scene changed to one of etheric beauty; one that I really cannot explain, due to the fact that this place is not of this realm. I found myself standing alongside another person whose aura I recognized as Dee! We were rather tall and slender beings with large heads with no hair and were wearing long silver flowing robes that went down to our feet (although I do not know if we even had feet, as I could not see them under the robes). Another thing I noticed was that neither of us were of any particular gender. We were neither male nor female in these bodies. This was the first time that I experienced something like this, or even thought about it. I also got the impression that we were not in a timeframe anywhere near our present timeframe here on Earth. I sensed that this was a long time away in the far future in another galaxy. Of course, when I told Dee about these adventures after we came back to the Earth Plane, she said, "Yes those people are the 'Tin' people that I encountered previously."

I countered that we were these people. Dee said "Why not? Why can't we be these people?" I thought about it for a minute and said, "I guess we could be." But, I said, "It felt like this was some future time for this to be happening"; however, I was reminded that there is no time, everything is really happening now. Time is irrelevant and not a factor in the scheme of things on a cosmic scale. Once again I was astounded by the amount of knowledge that Dee has at her fingertips, then again I should expect it from an old soul like hers.

Curiously, after this adventure into the future, I was transported back to the same American Indian scene that I had seen earlier. I was shown that I had been there before as part of that family. This was a quick little journey that I was grateful to have experienced as I completely enjoy new information about my past that I encounter, even if it is painful. Naturally, these are events that have brought us to where we are today since all of our past lives and history are part of us. We have experienced these things, and they collectively have made us who we are in the present. Remembering them affords us a valuable tool as to why we respond the way we do to incidents that occur today.

(7/1/2005)

Last night Dee and I, after several bouts with the healing Angels decided to merge for our own enjoyment. This is something that we have enjoyed before but lately, due to the work the Angels have been doing, anytime we decide that we want to merge, the Angels view it as an opportunity to jump in again for additional healing. They just do not understand about our free time or our need for them to back off for a short while. But last night, since they had already had several intense sessions with us, we decided to try. Dee said later that she had clicked out early, but I was able to enjoy the whole time. I let spirit take me anywhere that I needed to go. They chose to take me back in time once again to many previous lives that Dee and I had experienced together.

We started in the not too distant past, where we were some type of American Indian, but it felt more like Central or South American than North American. The timeframe I would guess to be around 1300-1500 A.D. I was sick at the time and lying on a bed of sorts, wrapped in clothes to keep my body warm. I don't know what precipitated these conditions, but I was very sick at the time. There was a medicine man dancing around in full regalia including a mask that looked like a duck face to me but was very elongated. Many vibrant colors were painted on the various crevices of the mask, and it had feathers dangling off it. I was not frightened because I was a sick patient being healed by the village shaman: however, being a traveler from another time I was a bit taken back by the whole scene. It was very curious how I could be participating in the scene as the sick party and as an observer at the same time. Sometimes these travels bring many different dimensions of oneself into the forefront without any prior knowledge, and it can create some very awkward feelings on the part of the person who is just coming into this scene. I do not know if the healing done at that time worked or not because I was transferred to another time very shortly. I think the purpose of this episode was to show me a time when Dee and I had been together previously, because she was the medicine man for the tribe. (She always seems to get the cool jobs.)

Movement in this realm is very quick and can be upsetting to the stomach on occasion, but I have come to tolerate those movements, and I no longer get that queasy feeling when it happens. When I did stop, I was on an Egyptian long boat. I am not sure of the proper name for these, but it was one of those boats that had many slaves rowing on the below decks. This was a ramming boat for battles. Looking about I saw Dee, as a man, a few rows down from where I was rowing. We were both exhausted and working hard to keep up the pace with the others. It seemed like we had been there for a long time, at least several months, and it appeared that we were going to be there until we died. How long from this point that would have been I do not know because I was moved from this location shortly after I took in the surroundings.

Upon getting my bearings once again I knew that I was now in pre-historic times. There were no buildings or roads around, just a few footpaths that people had to make their way through a tropical paradise. I came to a cave and went inside. There were several people, maybe eight or so, mulling around in there. I had some berries in my hands, and I continued towards the back of the cave until I came upon two other people, one man and one woman, who were painting on the walls of the cave. There was sufficient light, and it seemed as though it was artificial light, not natural light from a hole in the top of the cave. It did not occur to me at the time to investigate the light any further, although I now wish that I had because it might have proved informative on the lighting of caves during those times. I took my berries and mixed them together with several other types of berries and dirt like material to make a very satisfying color of magenta to paint the walls. I was tasked with painting a scene that showed how we had been able to kill a large animal for our group to utilize for survival. It seemed that this was a great honor to be able to paint this on the wall. I don't know why, but I believe it may have had to do with my participation in the bringing down of the animal for our use. The two others involved in the painting also seemed to have something to do with the animal too. I was starting to paint the wall with my story of how the animal was taken down, when I was again taken away and moved to another location.

Unfortunately, this was the end of my time there as I was brought back to the here and now. I had the feeling that I was going to go back even further in pre-history at this juncture; however, it didn't happen. I had not seen Dee at this cave dwelling so I don't know if she was there and I just missed her, or if I was in this life by myself. I tend to feel that she had been there somewhere although we did not interact at that particular time.

42

The Angel Team

The other day after one of our healing sessions with the Angels, Dee told me that she had met some of the members of the Angel team who were helping us with our healing sessions. She said that they were always in a circle surrounding us with their love during any of the healing times. I asked her, "Who are they?", and she said that some of them were new to her, and she did not know if they were just my Angels, or her Angels, or both of our Angels as we do share some of the same ones. She said that Madagascar was there of course, since she works with both of us and she has been with us since the start of the healing on Dee. Then there was Mega, Charlotte, Renald, Felicia, Micah and Jenra. Micah is one of Dee's Angels, and her job is to help people, such as us, to move along their spiritual pathways.

It never ceases to amaze me how Dee can just communicate with the Angels anytime she wishes. Just like with this circle. Dee communicated with them during one of our healing sessions. I am usually taken out of the situation so that it does not take a toll on my physical body. Dee can be getting healing done and at the same time have a conversation with the Angels as if she were talking to you or me in the physical. It is truly amazing and something to behold.

The Angels took me out of the process. They did not tell me they were doing it, it just happened. In fact, I did not even realize it until Dee asked me how I was feeling after a particularly harsh session. I immediately said to her that it was not a problem since the Angels had taken me out of the physical process. I didn't even think about that statement until later. Then I realized it. But Dee was not happy with my telling her that, so she had to ask them for herself, and they communicated the same message to her, that, I had been taken out of the process for my own well being.

This morning the Angels had found a new area to work on for Dee. So, like kids in a candy store this was new territory for them and they wanted to jump back in anytime they got the opportunity, which disrupted our lives. However, they are hard to turn down especially since they are helping us both. Anyway, this morning they just jumped in while we were holding each other and since this was an intense session, I should have been removed from it, but they said that we were not positioned properly for them to remove me from the situation. So I was left along for the ride during the short but heavy session. Dee asked me afterwards if I was okay. I said, "Yes." I then told her why that had happened. She had to laugh when I told her that we were in the wrong position, and then she said, "Well, if they would let us know when they were coming we would be able to align ourselves better for their benefit." I had to agree, but as I have said, the Angels are funny guys; they just want what they want, when they want it. They are like spoiled kids. We take this all with a sense of humor and gratefulness for what they are doing for us. We never get mad at them, even when they do jump in at inappropriate times.

(7/4/2005)

Today during a healing session I told Dee that someone was there. I meant that someone not usually present during a session had shown up. Dee said, "I saw him too." We do not discuss a person or any events that happen during a session until after it is over, because we do not want to shift the energy that is present or risk losing the connection. When the session was over, I said to Dee that the person or entity if you will, that had shown up was behind some kind of "wall", or something was in front of him because I could only see his face. She told me that the skin on the entity was very whitish in color. I interjected, "Yes like powder", and she agreed. She said that she could see ringlets for his hair that I could not see due to the fact that he had a hat on. Dee said she did not see the hat, but strands of hair falling down around his neck. I took this to be the fact that she saw the hair and I saw the hat. I also told Dee that I could see one white shoe that was projecting from the bottom of whatever he was standing behind. Dee then said she could not see a body, and I told her that was because he was standing behind something. Dee said his face had chiseled features that I could totally agree with. I saw a powered face and the features were subtler to me. Although I could see his eyes quite plainly, I did not know the color of them.

I find it very interesting when these things happen and when we can verify each other's view of things. I just get a great feeling because verification of what we see on these other planes does not come very often. When it does come, it just makes you feel better to know that one of us is seeing what they think they are seeing and not relying on imagination for some of the details. I have found that there is no imagination because whatever we conceive in our minds has to come from somewhere, and what we call imagination can also be from our higher selves.

(7/6/2005)

What a day we had today! It started out with a bad night at the firehouse because there were rainstorms and we were out helping people that were flooded and stuck in cars all night. When I got home I was dog-tired, but the Angels had other ideas for me. They started right in with one of their normal sessions, which wasn't too bad, but they did not stop there. They continued doing this for the whole day! I became completely wiped out from this, and I literally could not even stand up after a while. This was somewhat disconcerting, but I had this happen before so I understood the situation.

It got so bad that Dee called on Michael and asked him to tell them to stop for the day because they were taking too much out of me. She told me that she had asked him to just let us merge and leave us alone together for some time, and he said okay. I spoke to him myself later on in the day after we had the luxury of merging a couple of times, and he told me that we could merge once more today but then it was back to business. By the end of the day I was so totally exhausted that all I could do for the rest of the night was sleep.

THE ANGEL TEAM

(7/9/2005)

Today a new entity came into my view so I knew to expect something different. This was a large bluish entity with a long flowing blue robe. He just stood off to the side, but I knew that he was in charge and I expected the unexpected. Of course, that is what I received.

During the session I was hit with all of these extremely intense painful feelings. At first I did not know what they were doing, and then I remembered that I had asked for this. Dee did not understand because I was in such pain that I was literally crying out. She asked them to stop, and I could not tell her at the time that it was fine even with the pain that I was experiencing. For the past few weeks they have taken me out of any physical problems that may occur during a session by making me an observer. However, today I was in the role of a full participant. I did not realize why until they were finished. After the session was over, and I told Dee that I had asked for this, working on her physical pain, the Angels came back to me and shook my body loose of any of the pain that I had held. They explained to me that this pain from Dee had to be withdrawn from her and placed into my body, and then they would release it from my body when the session was over. This did not sit well with Dee. She does not like it when I experience the pain that is associated with her illness. I told her that if this was the way the Angels said it had to be, then that was fine with me because it was helping her. So what did the Angels do? Well, right after we got everything straightened out as to what was going on, they just jumped right back in, not for one more session, but two more sessions, one right after the other.

They just do not understand time, or the fact that my physical body needs a break sometimes; even though we try to explain to them. It simply goes right over their heads.

(7/12/2005)

Today the Angels decided to put my body on "hold" for a short period. They made my body immovable from my hips down to the bottom of my legs. Now mind you, they have done similar things before, such as making my legs immovable for a period of time. But, today was definitely different. My body was frozen in a position for well over an hour. I had never experienced anything like this. Not that I was worried, but it was a very long time to be immobile. When they finally released me from this traction like feeling, I asked Dee what the Angels had said about this because I had not gotten anywhere with them during the whole time, although I tried many times to communicate with them. Dee said that she had asked them all to release me, but they said it was necessary. Dee did not take that lightly, so eventually she called on Michael and Metatron to ask them to release me. She had no luck there either.

Finally, Dee called in the big guns; she called Yeshuah (Christ) and God Himself to unravel this mystery before her. She did not tell me at the time that she was doing this, I only found out afterwards (as usual), because most times during these events she and I are on different wavelengths communicating with the other side. Nevertheless, as soon as Dee called for the big guns, she said that I was immediately released from this immobile position. She thanked everyone for their help, and then told me what had happened. She knew from the beginning why I was immobile from the waist down. Earlier in the morning Dee had been in terrific pain from the waist down through her legs and feet. Apparently the Angels decided to do something about it. Since I was not up to speed for what they wanted to do, they had to adjust my body to the situation at hand. Therefore, I had to be immobile for the time period that they were doing their thing.

Soon after the adjustment with the Angels was completed, they jumped right in and had a session with Dee and I. At first I did not think anything unusual for this session, but very soon I found out that it would not be a "typical" session. As I wrapped my legs around Dee during the initial stages of the session, I immediately felt a lot of pain. Then I knew exactly what they were doing. From then on in, I experienced a terrific amount of pain from her legs and from her hips. She said, "Why don't they transmute it immediately so that I would not have to experience it directly?" I said that they told me they cannot do that, but when the session was over they would release the pain from my physical body. After about twenty minutes or so they were finished, and they did release the pain from my body. Dee said later on that people just do not realize the pain she is in on a constant daily basis. Well, I now understood some of the painful experiences that she goes through daily and I can tell you that they are very painful indeed.

I am so grateful to God and the Angels for these experiences I am having because they have made me aware of so much around me in this world. I see everything in such a different light now. I am much more patient with people, even those I do not get along with. I smile internally when I have to deal with people that I do not normally get along with, and they cannot figure out why I am not getting upset anymore, even when they try to get my goat. I just move on and send love to them because that is what they need the most. What I find the most interesting is their reactions when I decline to raise the bar when talking to them. I find that just going along and sending love to them is the best way to handle most of these situations.

43

A Day with the Angels

(7/13/2005)

Today I had another interesting adventure in "A day with the Angels"; however, there was a different twist. They merged Dee and me while doing their thing this morning. I felt the difference right away, and told Dee that we were merging along with the healing. I was unaware of any reason for them to do this, but it had a tremendous effect upon me. Merging together with Dee is a literal combining of our souls, and to have this done at the same time as the Angels were doing a healing process, just overloaded my bodily circuits. They literally did not know what to do. After the session was over and after I had transmuted all of Dee's pain from my body, the Angels told me that we were at a new level. I figured maybe this would be a part of the process going forward. Let me tell you something. I was hoping this was not the case because I was afraid I would have to stop at this point and not be able to continue if they were going to merge us all the time during a healing. It would be just too painful and too consuming to my physical body to do that.

I asked Dee if she knew what was going on. Thankfully she

did. Because as soon as I said to her during the process that we were merging, she went ahead and asked Madagascar, "What was going on?" Dee said Madagascar told her she (Dee) had been asking for time for us to merge lately without interference from the Angels. Madagascar had done that because Dee had been complaining that we don't get time enough for ourselves. Dee had to explain to Madagascar that we thank her for the opportunity to merge, but we cannot do that during a healing session due to the fact that it puts my physical body on overload, and I cannot be in such a state because it is too much for the physical body to tolerate at one time. You see, the Angels for the most part have no understanding of what a physical body is like, because most of them have never had one.

44

Healing

After Dee and I had recent incredible merging experiences instructed by the Angels, there had been a noticeable change in my body physically. You see, now, whenever I am apart from Dee, I begin to feel a physical aching in my chest. This is not just a longing for someone or something, this is pain. This pang I feel in my heart has a definable feeling and pain associated with it. I did not understand it when it first happened. I was at the firehouse and I began to feel this aching in my heart. I initially brushed it off, just as most of us do when something new develops within our bodies. We treat it as if it will go away in a short time if we simply ignore it. I instinctively knew that I had to merge with Dee. This desire became all encompassing throughout my shift at work. I had a definite pang in my heart that was palpable, and it had to be quenched! There was no way to do that at work so I was forced to bear it until Dee and I could be alone together.

I explained to Dee what I was feeling. She said that she thought that I was having these feelings all along, at least whenever we were apart, because she had been feeling these pangs from the beginning of our relationship whenever we had been apart!

This hit me hard because I had not experienced this type of feeling ever before in my life.

I have felt the normal missing of someone that you care about, but never had I experienced something like this. When Dee explained to me that she has been feeling this way all along it nearly blew me away, because I had no knowledge this even existed. Dee said she never mentioned it to me because she felt that I was experiencing the same feelings of loss as she was during these times. I told her that she forgets that I am new at this; I only started about six months ago. She is fully aware of this fact; she just naturally thought I was having the same feelings she was having, especially since we do connect readily in the Ether. This was an eye opener for both of us. I asked her to tell me whenever she feels something in her physical body. That way, we both would know that at least one of us is experiencing something new and different.

As usual, the Angels did not take long to act upon this new feeling that I was experiencing. The very next time that we merged something entirely magical happened. I was told that I was now at a high enough level that I could start to help Dee with her pain and her RSDS (Reflex Sympathetic Dystrophy Syndrome). RSDS is the cause for Dee to be totally disabled and have to take many medications daily just to function as a normal person. Naturally, this has bothered me from the beginning of our relationship. The fact that she is in such pain and I cannot help her with it is always on my mind.

Whenever we merged, I went through a crying phase because I could feel her pain and knew that I was helpless to do anything about it. All I could do was sob for a minute or two and then move on to the blissfulness that merging brought us both. When we merged and I was told that I could help her, I immediately told Dee she would be a part of any further adjustments that the Angels made to my body. In fact, I would be the conduit to help her improve her body! I was extremely excited about this. I found out later that Dee was questioning the Angels' methods. For now, I was excited about helping her to improve, even if it was in a small way. We went about our business of merging at the Angel's request, and what I found was that these new adjustments were going to make any previous adjustments seem like merely a warm up. However, I agreed to it, so the Angels were just living up to their side of the bargain. These new adjustments included holding Dee the entire time. I was advised that the longer that I could endure it, the better it would be for Dee. Therefore, I told myself that I would hold her as long as possible each and every time these adjustments were being done.

Dee asked spirit, "Why is my healing coming through Rich?" She was told, "This is what was agreed to in the contract". Thus, all of this was set up even before either of us were born, and we were supposed to be together now, and we are exactly where we are supposed to be. This rang a bell for me because it is the same question that Barbara asked me when she and I were working on my past lives a few weeks ago. I was given essentially the same answer-- which we are exactly in the place we are supposed to be at this time. There really are no coincidences.

With Dee's condition, she has very poor circulation in her lower legs and in her feet. She said that she has not been able to feel her feet since 1997 and her legs were always numb below the knee. However, after the first two sessions of adjustments for her through me, her lower legs began to get some feeling back! She said that she could feel the blood beginning to flow into that part of her body. I was so excited that I had to see for myself. So I took her feet, which were usually blue in color and cold to the touch, and I held them in my hands. I could not believe it, but they were actually pink in color and were warm to the touch. I knew this was real because I had been trying to help her for a long time by holding her cold feet and trying to heal them as best I could. Unfortunately, it had been to no avail. But now, actually looking at her feet and feeling the warmth in them was so exciting to me that I almost broke down and cried because I was just in awe of what God could actually do through Angels. Dee said she was beginning to experience feeling in her foot and she could actually bend some of her toes, something that she had not been able to do since the blood flow had been restricted for so many years. I found it hard to believe this was actually happening, and I was a part of it. I now was convinced that all of what I had been going through for the past couple of months had a purpose. The Angels were showing me what that purpose was. It was also to raise me up to a level so that I could help Dee with her condition. I cannot tell you how happy I feel to be able to help Dee -- even a little bit. I find myself feeling her feet to make sure that they are still warm all of the time. Dee says she now has some feeling in her feet, whereas she had none before.

While we were doing our now "normal merge/healing session", a most extraordinary thing took place. We were into a very involved session when all of a sudden I had to stop! Dee had to physically detach from me. I had to break the contact, and when I did, my body went into spasms because I interrupted the whole process, and the Angels did not like to be interrupted since they were working on us. After a few minutes of separation my body uncontorted itself, and I was able to regain control over my physical self. During these adjustments I really have no control over my body. I am not afraid of the adjustment and neither is Dee, except that sometimes something will occur that she is not expecting. That gives her a bit of a jolt due to the surprise of it, but otherwise she can deal with it without a problem. This time though we both knew that something was different. She asked, "Why did I feel that I had to stop when I did?" I told her at first that I did not know why, which was the truth. But after a few more minutes when my mental faculties caught up with me, I was told by the Angels what had happened. You see, I was very involved with Dee and her RSDS symptoms. I could literally feel her pain within myself, and knowing that I cannot relieve her from her pain; I got very emotional and cried through the portion of the pain that passed through me. Since this is such an intense feeling for me, the Angels were going to do us a favor. The Angels were going to give me her pain. They were going to have us both literally switch bodies. She would have the aches and pains that I experience, and I would have all of her pain that she deals with on a day-to-day basis. Please realize, I did not consciously ask them to do this nor did Dee. In fact, her first comment was that they couldn't do that. But, we both knew that was not the correct way to deal with her problems.

I just felt so badly that I could not help her with her pain. My higher self apparently took on the job of dealing with it for me. We both knew this would be wrong. And that is why we had to stop and disconnect when we did, because they were literally ready to switch our bodies out with each other. I felt very badly after this incident because I felt as if I had let Dee down. Dee told me we could not do what the Angels were prepared to do. She had to experience her pain for herself. I will just continue to help her the best way I can, and that is by letting the Angels do God's work through me to help heal Dee in the best way that they know how. I have come to the point that I do not second-guess the Angels, and I usually go along with what they say or do because they are generally correct with their actions. This particular time though, I did have to stop and let them know that even though their intentions were good, we could not follow through with it on their behalf. Both Dee and I are comfortable with our decision.

We continued with our sessions with the Angels, which were on a daily basis and even sometimes, were hourly occurrences. These new sets of adjustments last about an hour, and put a tremendous strain on me physically. However, I think they are working on that too. They came to me the other night and worked just on me for a period of time, and I was told that those particular adjustments were for me in order to make it easier for my physical body to withstand Dee's adjustments that I will be going through. I will have to see if their adjustments help me.

45

Grounding

(8/5/2005)

It's been a couple of weeks now, and I haven't had anything to write about. It's just that nothing has really changed. Dee and I go through our rituals sometimes four or five times a day with the Angels where I have been taking away her pain and letting it go from me as soon as they are finished with us.

Last night was a bit different in that I could sleep very little. I kept waking up after short intervals due to the tremendous pain that my body was in. In particular, my legs were killing me. First, my right leg was in great pain which is very unusual. The pain was all the way from my hip down the outside of my leg into my ankle and foot. I could not figure out why it hurt so much. I tried to think if I had hurt it or something, but I did not. So I tried some ointment that is really for arthritis and joint problems since it was the only thing that we had in the house. I tried it, and it actually seemed to take the edge off of the pain after about an hour.

Then about an hour later, I was again awakened by tremendous pain in my left leg! My right leg felt very good at this time, so I figured that since the ointment worked before, I would try it again. I put it on my left leg all along the outside down to my foot and hoped that it would work the same way. And, since my neck and shoulders were also aching (which is an almost common everyday affair), I decided to try it on those areas too. Again in about an hour my leg began to feel better, but my neck and shoulders felt the same as they had before I applied the ointment. At least I had some benefit from the ointment. I went back to sleep and was able to stay asleep the rest of the night, although it was already 3:30 AM at this point, and I had only gotten about two hours sleep the entire night.

When the morning rolled around, the Angels were right there to jump in again, and they did, as soon as we were both awake. Dee and I are used to it by now, and she is ready for the session anytime it happens. Many times we can tell when they are coming. They like to tug on my left arm with quick jerking motions, kind of like a dog tugging at you when he wants to go outside. Sometimes Dee can feel them herself when they are about to jump in, so it is not usually a great surprise when they do. But occasionally, they jump in without warning and just go to town with their moving and shaking and drawing pain from Dee into me. After this morning's session, I had released the pain that I had taken from Dee, and it occurred to me that during the previous night I had not given up the pain that I had taken in. Now mind you, I was really exhausted both in body and mind that day from all that had occurred during the previous 24 hours, but the Angels tried to jump in a couple of times. They were successful albeit for very short durations due to my physical and mental condition. I recalled that I did not let the pain go at all that day when they were through and that was probably why I was in such pain all night. Sometimes things just come to you out of the blue or, maybe it was the Angels telling me this. Suddenly Archangel Michael came to me with a big smile on his face. He did not speak to me. He was standing in the distance and all of a sudden he picked up a ball of bright light that was about the size of a bowling ball, he went into a bowling ball stance that one would do at a bowling alley, and he rolled the bowling-ball sized piece of light energy directly at me. The ball of light energy went directly into my head with an enlightening kind of feeling and Michael simply said, "You needed that". I said, "Thanks", which is all I could think of at the moment, mainly because I was rather stunned by the whole situation. Then Michael simply disappeared.

Although I was very tired, even haggard at this point, within a few minutes my strength came back and my thought processes cleared up dramatically. I thanked Michael again and, although he was now gone from my presence, I know he was aware of my thoughts for giving me a tremendous energy boost at a time that I really needed it. Angels are always watching over us, and they know what we need even before we know what we need. I just shook my head once again at this amazing process. It was going on all the time around not just myself, but around each and every one of us on this planet. We just have to be open enough to feel, listen, and hear them when they are contacting us.

I feel that Dee and I are entering a new faze of the healing process for her because whenever we are in a session with the Angels, I can literally feel myself drawing the pain from her body in any place that I am working on her with the Angels. I feel this pain very viscerally, and it does hurt a great deal sometimes, but as soon as the session is done, the Angels make sure that I disperse the pain from my body by some very heavy grounding procedures. I seem to have this grounding down pat but earlier in these sessions, I had trouble getting grounded. I would not be able to get back to the physical plane all the way. I would become stuck between here and there which was not a very comfortable place to be. When I was stuck between these two energy fields I would literally have to go outside and hug a tree. The tree hugging usually worked, but sometimes it would take five to ten minutes before I was all the way back to the Earth Plane. I don't recommend being between two planes because you can literally feel both places together, and they do not belong together; they are separated for a reason and to be in both dimensions at the same time makes for a really heady ride.

When I am working with Dee during a session we (meaning one or both of us) sometimes feel the pain level increasing, and we will exclaim "ouch" or some other expletive if it is warranted. We do not know how long or how intense these sessions will be, but many times these intense feelings come at unexpected times. When I feel that we are winding down, sometimes the Angels go off in an entirely different direction. What I mean by that is they may go to a different part of the body than they were working on before and start anew. Or, as often is the case, when we are finished and I have released the pain, they will jump right in and start again. These things happen all of the time, and I now realize why I have not been working more for these past several months. I am needed here at this moment, so this is exactly where I am. Dee needs me to be here, and the Angels need me to be with Dee while we are working together. Initially, it was me who needed to be brought up to speed with Dee but, since that time, I have been brought up to the proper vibrational level and I can now help Dee with her pain. The Angels have thought all this out, but they don't usually fill us in on what they are doing. We usually find out about things after the fact, and then we go back and assess the situation. What we find is that they knew what they were doing all along; they just did not fill us in as quickly as they should have. But, we have to accept them the way they are. It is pretty hard to argue with them, as Dee sometimes does when she feels that they are going too far or for too long a duration during a session. Sometimes they listen, and sometimes they don't. I guess we have a choice, either to do it or tell them that we won't do it, but since I made this contract long ago, I will go along with what they have set up for us. Besides, I could not be performing a better service than to be helping someone who is in real pain all of the time.

On a much brighter note, the other night Dee had a talk with God Yeah; she talks to God pretty much whenever she wants. I am still amazed at the things that she can do. Anyway, she's complaining to God that she and I have been working too hard lately and that the Angels don't let us have time to merge like we used to, and she would like us to have the opportunity to do that because it is such an enlightening experience. So what do you think happened? Later on in the night, the Angels wake us both up for a session, and we were able to merge as she had asked. I did not know anything about her talking to God or asking for what we received, but He did answer her pretty quickly, and she did thank Him for his promptness in allowing us that time together.

46

Overload

Today was interesting in that when Dee and I were working with the Angels we both fell asleep. When I awoke we were still holding each other, which is not a bad thing except that we were still in contact with each other -- meaning we still had a connection for the Angels to use to pull pain out of Dee and put it in me, and to transfer energy from me to her. Due to this contact my body received an overload of transmission from Dee. The Angels do not understand that there are physical limits to what a physical body can withstand at any given time. This caused me a great deal of physical pain. I had such tremendous pain in my legs that I could not move them. This happened once before and that was not a good situation either. But this time, my legs were aching severely. I told Dee about this, and she said that she had already been asking Metatron and Michael to help me. Unfortunately, they said that they could not help me with this particular situation and that it would have to work itself out. I was pretty much on my own! The pain at times became so severe it caused me to cry several times as the pain shifted from one area of my legs to another. Ultimately the pain did subside, and I was able to release the rest of it in my normal way. However, this took the better part of an hour to accomplish, and I was not in very good shape when it was all over.

I have learned something from this little adventure and that is we should not fall asleep while holding each other since the angels might continue working, and I could end up in this situation again. Usually, I allow them to work until I cannot take the pain anymore and then I consciously disengage so that I can release the pain without too much trouble. Also, my body is not wiped out by a session if I cut it off when my body is "full". Sometimes they will end a session themselves without any fanfare, but on occasion they will continue with no end in sight. It is at those times that I have to consciously step in and take myself out before we go too far.

Another thing that happened last night was that someone new came into the picture. I mentioned this to Dee during the session and indicated that she should look for somebody different. Usually she can pick up on a new person in some form. Sometimes Dee will get the impression first, occasionally, neither one of us will get a good picture until sometime later. Today I was able to see this whole person. It was a man dressed like a king. He was decked out in flowing regal clothes, had a full beard, and wore a crown. He had a wonderful smile on his face. He did not say anything; he was just there observing the session. I got the impression that Dee and I were on a new plane of healing, indicating that new entities will now be showing up. The king may very well be a part of that next phase.

After the session was over I asked Dee if she had seen the person. She said that she only saw someone with something large on his or her head, but she did not get a clear picture. I explained to her what I saw, but she indicated that she had only gotten an impression. As I said before, sometimes we are able to see the same things and sometimes only partial identities of different entities.

It is very strange when a new entity comes into view during a session. It is at first difficult to feel if this is a new being or someone that has been here before. I can feel someone or somebody coming into the group, but it is difficult to try to place the energy initially. But, when I begin to feel that the new entity has a different energy, then I know that it is someone new. When I tell Dee about it, and she looks for the new energy, she can tell if it is someone new or if it is someone we already have had contact with. If I feel that the energy is different, we are very curious as to why this being is here and where it came from. Usually they are forthcoming and tell us all we want to know, but sometimes they are on a different vibrational level and communication is not the easiest thing to do. But we do our best and at least get some idea.

We find this part of the experience the most fascinating because we have met and been introduced to beings from many parts of the Universe. Some are not in the physical, and others are just beings from other planets that are just a part of the whole picture of the Universe. They are playing their part in showing us that there really are other planets and civilizations out there and that we can contact them if we look in the right places. Dee can usually talk to these entities at her leisure, but this being was a bit standoffish and did not speak to either Dee or myself. This did not offend me, as many beings are not very talkative on many occasions. I was too involved with the healing session myself to be able to try to connect with this being, but I could sense his presence. Dee did not try to speak to him either. At the proper time I was sure that he would come forward. For now I was content that he was there as we have sensed a change in the vibrational level. So, whatever his mission is, we feel he is there to help us. We accept all new comers and we thank them for their help. A thanks is a very important aspect of this process, as it should be whenever someone does us a favor.

Dee hollers at the Angels when they go too far with me, as when the session lasts an extra long time or when it is a very intense session and they are creating a lot of pain for me. I tell her that it is okay because when it gets too intense for me I just let it go and come back to this plane. Then I release the pain, and I usually feel all right. They do sometimes hurt my left shoulder, but I can't really blame them for that, because my left shoulder had been previously injured in an incident at the Fire Department and will continue to give me pain for the rest of my life. They just bring the pain level up a few notches. As far as I am concerned, this is very minor as long as we can keep on working to bring Dee back to full health because she has been suffering for eighteen years.

47

Lily Dale

Lily Dale is the seat of Spiritualism in the United States and is the home of the National Association of Spiritualist Churches (NASC). The town is extremely interesting, and a wonderful place to visit since many mediums reside there, particularly in the summer. In fact, the Pastor of our church has a home there, as well as other members of our church. The church we attend is called The Journey Within and is a Spiritualist Church affiliated with the Spiritualist's National Union (SNU) in England. Unlike most of the major religions, Spiritualism does not tie its adherents to a creed or dogma. Our church has a set of principles which act as guidelines for the development of a personal philosophy of how to live your life. These principles are as follows:

The Fatherhood/Motherhood of God; The Brotherhood/ Sisterhood of Man; The Communion of Spirits and the Ministry of Angels; The Continuous Existence of the Human Soul; Personal Responsibility; Compensation and Retribution Hereafter for All Good and Evil Deeds Done on Earth; and Eternal Progress Open to Every Human Soul.

TALKING WITH ANGELS

(8/19/2005)

We have just returned from Lily Dale. It was such a nice experience, very peaceful and serene. There was a beautiful lake and a feeling of warmth and belonging in the whole area. Dee took some terrific pictures too. One of them by the lake has a very active spirit in the picture.

During the session with the Angels last night I felt an unusual pain that I had not felt before. It was located in my left hand. I had my hand on Dee's back and my fingers felt as if they were each attached to a nerve in her body. I was getting direct current from these nerves flowing through my hand and arm. This was a very severe pain, one that I was feeling directly through my hand, through my lower arm, and up and through my shoulder. I don't know how long that pain was sustained, but when I could not tolerate it any more, I had to stop the session. Afterwards, when it was all over and I regained my composure, I asked Dee if she had felt the pain too. She indicated that she had and understood the pain I was feeling. Later that night, as I knew it would, my shoulder literally woke me up because of the pain. This usually happens when I get a workout on my left shoulder or whenever I use the shoulder a lot. I was not prepared for the intenseness of the pain though, because I was literally awakened from a sound sleep.

(8/21/2005)

Tonight, during a dual back-to-back session with the Angels, I experienced some very pointed knifelike pains darting through my body. The best part was that when they were finished, and I was releasing the pain from my body, I saw an Asian Indian woman. She was sitting on what looked like a two-step platform that led to a wide-open area. She had large black almond-shaped eyes and jet-black hair, which tumbled down her shoulders. She was dressed in an orange and maroon Sari that went down to her feet, and she was wearing sandals. Her dress was all sequined, very ornate with a top front piece in a rectangle that was bejeweled and had a bird with large plumage on it. It was in many different hues of blue and green, and it seemed like there was a reason for her being there but the encounter was so brief, and flashed by so quickly, that I could not get an impression of her purpose in that setting. Immediately after that encounter the Angels stopped, and she was gone. I will remember her, and if I see her again, I will attempt to find out her purpose and I might learn a thing or two in the process. I plan to seek her out because she was very intriguing and alluring. This was the first time that I came across an Indian woman of this sort.

Yesterday, I had a talk with Michael, Gabriel, Metatron and Archangel Sandalfon (the brother Archangel to Metatron and the "Archangel of Prayer and Heavenly Music") and since then they have been behaving themselves and given Dee and me some peace and time to just be together without interruptions. We'll have to see how long this lasts. They are supposed to make some changes in the sessions around Labor Day as they did in the past. What that means is that I will just have to wait to see how the sessions change from what they are now. Dee has been yelling at them that they had better take me out of the process again, as they did before this current set of sessions began. She, as well as I, asked on several occasions during these sessions if I could be taken out but the answer has always been "No". So, we will just have to wait until the next changes take place to see where I will be at that time.

(8/22/2005)

This is Dee's perspective on a few of the Angels' healings that we have experienced:

During healing with Rich, I was observing ancient Egypt... on the shore of what appeared to be a river. I could see the sand and the edge of the water very clearly along with two men dressed in the attire of those times. They were discussing the bloodline of the kings of Egypt, and each was holding what looked like vials of blood. They explained that before it was not pure, had been watered down (this is my impression), but that now it had been cleaned of the impurities and was pure once again. They then proceeded to pour the blood into the sand and into the water of the river until the vials were empty. I know there was more to this vision and more conversation, but that has not come back to me. I have to be honest, and say I don't quite understand what they were trying to get me to understand. But, as always, there is a reason for everything, and maybe they will show me, or Rich, just what it is they are trying to convey. In some way, I believe they were showing me my own health problems, and by our work with the Angels that slowly what has been done to my physical body will turn around. This I have never had any doubt about, as I have always had faith that one day I would be healthy once again, and free of pain. Although, a little confirmation from time to time never hurts!!

(8/24/2005)

During another healing session I was shown a group of Angels, that Rich and I were supposed to be with, but at what point in our lives I'm not sure. I explained it to Rich, and he somewhat understood, and helped me to understand. The Angels were a kind of transport group. They were transporting those souls who were not "nice". I saw them as depicted with shackles or bonds upon their hands, and walking in line, and as we arrived at the destination, the shackles were removed and they were set free. Rich interpreted this as: we were helping them to move forward in their spiritual evolvement. Sort of like what is done in soul retrievals, just a little different. This also goes along with something I was told a very long time ago by my Angels-- that Rich, Karen, and I were Savers of Souls. At the time I had absolutely no idea what they were talking about. In a way, I still don't.

(8/25/2005)

In the morning the Angels decided to have back to back healing sessions, probably because I was at work the day before. These were long sessions, which is a bit unusual for them. Then, later on in the evening, they were back again for three back-to-back sessions but of moderate length. At the end of the second session, since it was lengthy, Dee decided that it was enough, and she just let go. Usually she waits until they are done and I let go,

217

but she was impatient with them and decided to let go first. This was unusual, and I think that the Angels were baffled at what had just happened. With that sudden disconnect I think they were lost. But, I believe the Angels had other ideas on how to avoid this from occurring again.

During the last session something out of the ordinary happened. I was trying to say something, but I could not get the words out. During these healing sessions I sometimes say words that have no meaning to me or to Dee, we suppose it is some language that the Angels use, but we are not sure. However, during this session, I was trying to say something but my mouth just would not cooperate. I kept trying, and Dee knew I was trying to say something, but she had no idea what it was either. This became very frustrating to me as time went on, and Dee told me not to worry about it. Then I said, "No, it is important", and I kept trying to get the words out. This had never happened before, and I was trying my darnedest to say whatever the words were just so that I could finish the session. Most times when I do say words during a session I do not remember what they are afterward, mainly due to the fact that I am bilocated at the time and not all of my mind is functioning at the same level. After awhile during this session, I became so frustrated that I tried to start saying just the letters of what it was that I was supposed to be saying. Even this was very protracted and difficult for Dee to try to understand because I knew what I wanted to do, but she did not, and I was unable to communicate my intension to her directly. She tried to understand the letters, but it was just not working!

By this time, Dee knew that I was trying to communicate something to her, and as usual she tried to protect me and not let the Angels have their way, but it was to no avail. I continued to try to say words to Dee. She told me to calm down and not to worry about it. I told her that it was important. This seemed to change the dynamic a bit. Since I was able to communicate with Dee verbally, I was able to get the syllables out of my mouth for Dee to hear. There were several of them that I needed to say. I had no idea the purpose of these syllables, but I said them as distinctly as I could. Dee listened to all of them. When I was done getting them all out, I said to Dee that the Angels wanted her to repeat these syllables herself out loud. Don't ask me why, this is just what I was told to do. Dee tried to repeat the syllables that I had said but there were too many to remember, especially since she was not told to remember them prior to me saying them. So, I had to repeat them for her slowly and several times so she could understand what it was that I was saying. These syllables were not in English, so it made the repetition of them all the more difficult.

After a healing session, I usually do not remember what happened, except for brief snippets here and there. The same went for today. I tried to put together what I remember of what I was saying so that you get some idea. It sounded like the following: TU – NA – RA – MA – NA – RISH – TU, or something like that. It is as close as I can remember. Dee also does not remember what happened for the same reason that I cannot remember, we are both between two planes during these sessions, and what happens does not always translate to the here and now accurately.

Maybe we should start to tape the sessions. There apparently was a reason why Dee had to say these syllables, but the Angels are usually very cryptic when it comes to answering direct questions.

Today, after two very turbulent sessions in the morning, Dee was up, and I was just exhausted and lying down, when all of a sudden the Angels started up again with just me. This had never happened before. Dee heard the commotion that I was making and came over by me and realized what was happening, so she joined right in and we continued with another session, albeit it was shorter than the previous ones that we had been having. During this particular session, I wondered what was going on. I asked Madagascar what the deal was with me having a healing session and not being close to Denise. Madagascar said, "It is no longer necessary for you to be together for a session, and the Angels can perform one with just you alone." At the time during the session, I did not ask anymore questions as it is very difficult for my mind to be in two places at once, never mind trying to remember what happened during the whole episode.

But when the healing session was over, I explained to Denise what I had been told by Madagascar. Needless to say, she was not too happy with that. Dee feels this was just another way of controlling me, as they have tried to do in the past without my telling them that it was okay. I thought about it and realized that Dee was right; they should not do that unless there was an important reason to do so. Later on I told this to Madagascar, and she seemed to understand what I was telling her.

Then it dawned on me... this was why the previous night, they had Denise repeat the words that I was trying to say, and why

I felt it was very important for her to say them at the time. This was apparently fine for them to do solo healing sessions when we were not together. Crafty little "Angels" aren't they? I feel this was done due to the fact that Denise had let go earlier than they had wanted during a previous session, and they were just trying to figure a way around that from happening again.

48

New Entities

(8/29/2005)

This night as I was in the midst of a healing session with Dee, I suddenly found myself being taken up and out of this world, into deep space. This happened very quickly, and I had no idea where it had come from. From all of the various things that I experienced this did not particularly hit me as anything much out of the ordinary. I just went along for the ride to see where I was being taken. I find it always exciting when I go into outer space because I can be sent literally anywhere in the galaxy, and there are many extremely interesting places to go.

This turned out to be a quick trip to the stars, because as soon as I started to look around to try and get my bearings, someone came from the right side of my body and just jumped right into me! This happened so quickly I did not even get the opportunity to see who or what it was that had done this. I was immediately sent soaring back to the Earth Plane and back into bed with Dee. It took a few seconds for me to comprehend what exactly had happened, but when I realized I was back in my bed I felt good.

The next thing I had to deal with was, who or what had done

this to me and what was their intention. While this was happening to me I was involved in a healing session with Dee. This does take some getting used to, being moved around from one place to another, especially when you do not know when it will happen. When these strange events do occur, I try to keep calm because I know that no harm will come to me. By the same token, when another entity jumps into your body, it certainly gets your attention right away!

As soon as I was able to focus on this entity that was with me, I realized this was for Dee's benefit and, therefore, I was okay with it. There was a mental awareness from the entity that joined with me. I knew it was a male entity, but from where or for what exact purpose, I did not know. I only knew that he was there to be helpful. Right after my thoughts of why he was here, he tried to answer me but to no avail. You see, he was on a much higher vibrational level than me, and he just could not get down far enough for me to communicate with him. I immediately told Dee that there was another entity with us as soon as I could after he had jumped in. I did this to make her aware that something different may occur. I also let her know so she can try to either see or feel this entity. I can get some verification or she can communicate with the entity herself and find out where they are from and what their purpose is. The entity tried and tried to get me to communicate. However, I was nowhere near the vibrational level of this entity, so I had to just let go and let them do whatever they needed to do on this occasion.

Afterwards, when we had finished with the session, I asked Dee if she was able to get any information from the entity that I was not able to get. Sometimes, in a session, either one of us will pick up on a new entity and the other gets some information. Many times Dee will tell me that this or that happened, or that I was talking to her or to someone else, and I have no recollection of the conversation at all. I guess our minds can only handle a certain amount of input before we go into overload status, and parts of our brain shut down to allow other parts more access to where they need to be at a particular moment in time.

(8/30/2005)

After several intense episodes last night I could not sleep. My legs were in terrible pain, and I could not get comfortable. Things like that had happened before but this night the pain was incredible. Earlier in the evening, I had released as much pain as possible, and I thought I had gotten rid of it adequately, but apparently not, so I had to contend with it during the night. I took some Aleve for muscle pain and eventually they began to feel all right. Dee gets mad at the Angels when this occurs because she does not want me to be feeling additional pain. She feels it is at her expense. I do not mind when this happens, although I do try to avoid it. And, whenever it does happen, I take it in stride and do not put any blame anywhere. I just feel that it is part of the process, and I can deal with it.

Of course, this morning the Angels had to have their say, and they kept coming back for more and more. Right after we would finish a session, they would come right back to do an encore. They even did a session when we were not together, which shows you how desperate they had become. Then, another session was necessary while we were sitting on the couch having coffee. Finally, they ceased and desisted from any more. During this "break" time though neither of us could touch the other one because we were still too connected and the Angels would have jumped right back in again and we wanted to avoid that for a time. After a short while Dee wanted to go lay down again and, of course, as soon as we did, the Angels started again, but this time I think we both fell asleep due to the fact that we were both exhausted. We slept well and when we woke, we were refreshed and ready to move on to another day.

(9/2/2005)

A couple of days ago during a healing I noticed some entity come into the session. I mentioned it to Dee, as I usually do, to alert her to a new party. I usually have to wait until the session is finished, and then Dee will tell me who or what it was, and what she learned from the entity. What she said she saw was rather different than the norm. Dee said as soon as I said that someone joined us, she saw a knight in shining armor on a horse that also had full armor. She thought that it was rather strange. She had no communication with the entity and did not know the reason for his being there. No explanation came from him or anyone else at the time either. She said that he did not appear to be participating in the healing. We had to chalk it up to one of those odd occurrences.

The next day during healing I sensed another entity coming into the session, but again, I had no idea who or what it was. Afterwards, when Dee told me about it, she said that it was a regal man with long gray hair and a beard who reminded her of a king. She said his name was Richard. Dee also said she could not see any royal robes or anything of the sort. I said I had seen a king during a session a couple of weeks ago who was dressed in royal robes but, if I remember correctly, I could not see his face at that time. This royal person was involved in the session, but I do not know the full reason for him being there.

Last night was another rough night for both of us as I was having terrible pains in my legs, which kept waking me up. Eventually the pain eased so that I could sleep. Dee was awakened later in the night with a feeling of being terribly cold. She had to get up and wrap herself with blankets, but she was still cold. After awhile she was able to warm herself enough to try to get back to sleep. But, when she came back to bed, she woke me up and when I touched her she was really hot! She noticed it also but told me that she could not get warm enough just a few minutes earlier.

During one of these evening Angel sessions a woman came in and said that her name was Gwendolyn. Dee spoke to her, but I was too involved in the healing. I can sense someone entering, and I usually do not attempt any communication with him or her. I just tell Dee that someone entered, and leave it to her to find out any information that they may have for us. When Gwendolyn came in and Dee spoke to her, she said that she was here to do the work that her mate had not done on a previous occasion. Gwen went on to say that Charles, her mate, was sometimes a prankster. Dee did not understand what she was talking about until Gwen said the following: Charles was the man that was here previously on the horse with shining armor on himself and the horse. This surprised Dee, but Gwen said, "He is just a practical joker, and when I want something done right, I usually end up doing it myself." She was here today to complete the job that Charles was supposed to do when he showed up. This just keeps getting more interesting all the time. We have now encountered spirit entities who are also practical jokers. Gwen hung around most of the night with us, although we had no further communication with her.

Today was also different because the Angels have kept at least part of their bargain by not having me feel Dee's pain once my body absorbs it. Not that I don't believe them when the Angels say that things will change, but exactly what and how remains to be seen. However, for now we were both happy that I did not have to go through the process of releasing the pain once it is absorbed. Apparently, the pain is now flowing right through my body as a conduit and not stopping in my body to be released later.

We decided to go to Sedona in a few days to start checking out the area for a place to retire in a couple of years. We wondered what kinds of changes that may bring to our Angel sessions.

49

Sedona

(9/11/2005)

What a fabulous place we found Sedona to be! It was one of the most beautiful places that we had been. We found the mountains and the red rocks to be breathtaking and to have a very peaceful and calming effect on our bodies. We toured many of the well know sites, took lots of pictures and stayed in a cabin complex in the woods along the Oak Creek Canyon. The trees and the water running through the woods were just a wonderful site to behold. We could not get to all of the places or do all of the things that we wanted to do, but we knew that before we went there. This was just an exploratory trip to get acquainted with the area and to see if it spoke to us. The only disappointment we found was that the rainy season, which is usually in August, had extended into the first couple of weeks of September. We had one afternoon and evening of rain, but what was really disappointing was the fact that the humidity was up in the 60's plus range for most of our stay. The humidity, or really the lack thereof, is what we were going there to experience to see if it would have a good effect on our bodies. Humidity similar to that in New Jersey is what we wanted to avoid. The locals told us that this was unusual and that at times (outside the rainy season) the humidity is down to 20% or less. I guess we will just have to go back again at another time to experience it. We will try to go back sometime in January or February. We were advised that they do get winters there but not like New Jersey with all the snow and cold weather. Sedona only gets to maybe 30 degrees at night and the days are usually in the 50's during the winter. That certainly sounded good to me.

We spoke to many people, most of whom had moved there from somewhere else. We were told about places to move that were not quite as expensive as Sedona proper but with all that we had to do, we were not able to check any of those out this time around. We did collect a lot of information, and found out a lot about Arizona itself. The next time we will try to go for a longer period and investigate some of the other areas we were told about.

As far as the sights we did see, many red rock sites that have been acknowledged as spiritual, either by the white man, Indian or both, duly impressed us. Upon arriving from the South, as you do when approaching Sedona from the Phoenix area, the first site you come upon is Bell Rock, which looks exactly like a bell. This is purportedly one of the very spiritual rocks to be encountered and one that you can easily walk around the entire circumference without too much difficulty. We wanted to visit this rock in the early morning with the sun coming up to see the effects of sunlight at different times on the surface of the rock. We were not disappointed. The rocks look pure red in the early morning sun and they give off a spiritualness that is palpable. Just being in the area gives you a feeling that God is all around.

We drove up to Shnebly Hill by way of a dirt road. I don't know if we were supposed to take our rental car, but we made it there and back without too much difficulty. When we told some locals about it, they said that if your car made it up Shnebly Hill, then we would not have any difficulties with the other dirt roads that we would encounter in the area. The view from atop Shnebly Hill was a sight to behold. We could see for probably a hundred miles to some very distant mountain ranges. We looked down on the whole town from there, and we could identify all of the different rock layers in the earth. When one speaks of the awesome power of God, one need not look further than the truly grand vista presented before you on this peak. You have to be careful while taking pictures close to the edge because there are no fences to prevent you from slipping off into eternity a bit sooner than you may want to.

Another site we visited was Montezuma's Well. It is an ancient site that people have been using for more than a thousand years as a source of drinking water as well as for irrigation. It was a most interesting site. There were rock wall dwellings on the sides of this great crevice that we could not believe people had actually lived in since there was no way to get to it, except by dropping a rope or a ladder down the side of the wall and crawling down to the dwelling. I'm sure they must have been very hardy people to live in such conditions, especially willingly. I guess severe times made for extreme measures. We supposed they lived here to be safe from other tribes. Survival was the paramount thought on everyone's mind, and to take up arms against another tribe who were just trying to survive is almost beyond comprehension. But then again, we do similar things today for no good reason than we don't like what others believe, don't we? I am hoping that we learn someday that we are all here together and by joining together we will get a lot closer to God than by fighting amongst ourselves all of the time.

At this site there was also a "pit" dwelling. This is a house that was made by digging into the ground about six feet and constructing a house. You reside a few feet below the surface. These people were around about a thousand years ago. When we approached this particular pit, which was all that remained of the dwelling, I did not notice anything unusual. But, after Dee had taken several pictures, and we had walked around the foundation, I was suddenly hit with a very intense feeling of dizziness. I just stood there for a few moments and told Dee what was happening. I had to place my arm on the railing nearby and hold on so that I would not fall over. I had this intense feeling that I was about to experience something from another time, but another couple pulled over from the road and started to walk to the site. I then experienced a flash that what was about to happen was not to be shared with this other party and immediately I was brought back to the here and now with no dizziness or odd feelings. Then, I had the thought that I am supposed to come back to this spot again in the future, and I will be told something of my past. So Dee and I left this area for the time being but plan on returning to it on our next visit to the Sedona area.

SEDONA

(9/13/2005)

We arrived home late last night around one thirty in the morning and were dog-tired from our flight and the time change. We went to bed and slept soundly. By the way, we slept very well every night in Sedona too, which is unusual for us, and we were both pleased at that. Usually Dee or I am up many times during the night for one reason or another. It was truly a pleasure for both of us to sleep the entire night for several nights in a row. It must have been the area we were in, with the trees and the river and the red rocks all around that made our souls calm down each night for a full-nights rest. That was something that neither of us had anticipated happening, but we were very pleased that it did. Then, the Angels surprised us with a new experience while doing a healing. When they started it felt almost like Dee and I were merging, so I took a little time to try and recognize the feeling and see if I could determine what was happening. This was a very good feeling by the way. It went on for a period of time, and I thought this was something new that the Angels were doing. After they finished, I asked Dee if she noticed any difference in the healing. She acknowledged that there was a definite difference. She said, "Yeshuah told her that we would experience a change after Sedona." I replied, "Well, let's hope that this was a permanent change and not something that only happened this one time." The next healing session was the same as this previous one, and since then they are all of similar ilk. I was hoping that this was a new stage for her healing, and that we got some real tangible results from it.

I have been having an ongoing discussion with Archangel

Michael about, what seems to me at least, the slow progress that we are making in regard to Dee's health. We have seen definite and tangible results so far, especially regarding her feet, which used to be cold and blue with no feeling in them all the time. Now they are pink and warm and some of the feeling has come back into them. We are grateful for these changes but now, since we have been doing this for a couple of months, we would like to see more results. To me a step in the right direction would be a lesser amount of medicine that she has to take on a daily basis. This has been my pet peeve with Michael for quite some time. Since Angels do not recognize time, they think that just because they say something good is happening or will happen it does. However, the timing to Dee and I is another matter because it seems long. This morning Dee said that her ankles were not burning anymore, which they had been doing ever since she got feeling back in her feet. Dee also said that she has noticed a slight lessening of pain throughout her body ever since we came back from Sedona. I am keeping my fingers crossed and praying that even these small improvements will continue. This is what I am fervently praying for, that eventually she will get better and can live a full life without the pain that she has been experiencing for the past eighteen years.

(9/15/2005)

Yesterday Dee told me about a conversation that she had with Madagascar. I have not been feeling well these past few days due to the awful weather that we are having. My sinuses were in terrible shape. Dee decided to ask Madagascar if she could do some healing work on me. Dee said that this seemed to baffle Madagascar, and she could not figure out what Dee was asking. Dee said that this went on for a little while and at one point Madagascar said to Dee, "It's not supposed to work that way" meaning Dee was not supposed to heal me but that I was supposed to heal her. Sometimes it's apparent that the Angels just cannot relate to this physical reality. But, it was a nice gesture and I was thankful that Dee did try. We also got a good laugh out of it too. Baffling the Angels was a new experience. I guess they have one mindset, and until that work is accomplished, they cannot deal with anything else.

50

Changes

(10/6/2005)

Dee and I experienced a change regarding the Angels in the past couple of days. They usually just grab us and tug on my left arm, or Dee begins to feel dizzy. However, this was something new. The Angels have been tugging at our hearts and not letting go! Even after we let them have their way, and have at least two sessions in a row, they still are clinging to each of our hearts afterwards. This has lasted for the entire day for the past couple of days. Dee suggested that I ask Madagascar what was going on. I did ask and all she said was that this is the way it was going to be for a couple of days. You never really get a good answer from them when you ask direct questions. She also told me that after these couple of days things would change. Of course, she did not say what would change. So, we had our answer, not that we were satisfied with it, but it was the only answer I was given. Two days went by with their constant tugging, and then I noticed a change.

It started out as a normal session and then I noticed someone coming in. This is not unusual, but I did notice that this entity came in with a "Ta-Da!" -- meaning that "Okay I'm here, and *now* we can get started." It was more than a little strange. He certainly wanted to be noticed and remembered. When the session was over, I asked Dee about the entity who came in, and she knew who it was. Many times when I see someone or something happening during these sessions I only get a piece of it, and many times it does not coincide with what Dee sees or experiences, but this time they matched perfectly. I asked her what she experienced, and she started to answer by saying, "This entity just walked right in", but I interrupted and said, "Yes, this entity walked in like he owned the place and was ready to start right in since he was now here." She said, "Yes, that is what I also experienced." I told Dee that was all that I could remember, but it was very definite. I asked her what she had seen, and she told me she had seen someone come in with this dashing air wearing a full-length blue suit of clothing like a racecar driver. When I asked her who it was, she said, "At first I didn't recognize him, but then I realized it was Michael!"

Dee had seen Michael on the previous day, and he was wearing a knight's body armor and a tunic like a Roman soldier would wear. She saw him, and he said, "Don't you recognize me by now?" He changes his appearance so often that it is difficult to recognize him unless you know that he is coming. Today she did recognize him faster even though he was wearing completely different attire. She asked him why he was here today, and he told her that it was necessary for him to be there for "strength".

This was the change that Madagascar told us about the previous day. This was the first time that the Angels started to work directly on Dee's back. Not only did they work on her back, but they also put *my body* into direct contact with hers -- meaning that she felt that my back and her back were connected as one. Since we were connected in the same location the Angels must have felt that they could do more than they usually do during a session. Therefore, this turned out to be an extra long session and an especially strong one. I was subjected to Dee's pain flowing from her body into mine. This was okay though, because the pain was just flowing through my body and out again, it was not staying with me to be released later. This new experience was quite dramatic for us in that we were dealing with localized pain for the first time. My back acted as a direct conduit for the pain flowing outward from Dee. The pain then went down my legs and exited through my feet and, even though the pain was very intense, it was immediately released through my feet, and I was not in discomfort for a long period of time.

(10/8/2005)

Dee and I had a discussion about the recent changes in our healing sessions. She said she was feeling a change in that her emotional feelings were beginning to come into play during the healings. I told her that the Angels did say that things would change and that may be part of it. A short time later, a healing session began and I noticed a different feeling right off the bat. It is hard to describe the difference, but it was something that I could just feel. It was like separateness from the feelings of drawing pain from Dee or just having energy flow from her to me. I felt distanced from the process. I soon began to feel emotionally involved with the process, and then it dawned on me that the Angels were drawing emotional feelings from Dee through me and out into the world. Upon realizing what was happening, I was comfortable with the changes. The feeling eventually felt like a stream in the dead of winter where the water is flowing underneath a layer of ice. You know the ice is part of the stream but, at the same time, it isn't. That is the way I described it to Dee, and she understood. It wasn't an unpleasant feeling; it was just one of being an observer of the flow and not a participant per se. Afterwards, my legs were throbbing from all of the work that we had been doing for about an hour's time. This again was unusual and different; the time frame of each session is usually fifteen to twenty minutes. We were able to survive the longer session with little ill effects. Dee said that the session was very dramatic in that she knew what they were doing, and the feelings were just flowing from her body into mine. I did feel some of these dramatic events, but I was spared from most of the feelings that were passing through me at that time.

(10/27/2005)

I was getting a bit disturbed by not seeing any real improvements in Dee lately, even though we had been working with the Angels on a daily basis. I expressed this concern to her, and she surprised me by telling me all of the benefits that have come from our endeavors with the Angels. She stated that her feet are now always warm; she has much less cramping in her legs; and her entire body burns much less than it had. The burning sensation

CHANGES

to the skin is one of the most painful parts of the RSDS disease process. It makes any touching or brushing up against her skin an extremely painful experience.

Another major improvement for Dee has been that she now has moderate use of her right arm. Now I can touch her arm and hold her hand without it being a painful process. Her lower back is in less pain too. These items may seem like minor improvements but to anyone who is familiar with RSDS, these changes are tremendously beneficial. I thank all of the Angels, especially Archangel Michael who has been a very major player in this process, for all of their help and assistance.

Speaking of Michael, the other day after finishing a healing session, an Angel literally took possession of my body and gave me a very intense session of my own. At the time I did not know who it was or why they were doing it. I was not afraid because I knew intuitively that it was involved in the total healing process, but it was different than anything that I had experienced. This was not like an ordinary adjustment. Dee realized this, don't ask me how, and she immediately began to holler at the Angels and told them to stop what they were doing. Of course, they ignored her pleas, but she continued to chastise them anyway. When it was all over and done with, I explained that my body had been taken over by an Angel, but Dee had already known that, and that was why she was angry. Then, Dee asked Michael, "What was going on?" and he told her that they were "raising the bar". That was all he told her. When she said that to me, it made sense because the process felt completely different from anything that had been done to me previously. This did not make Dee feel any better but it did at least present a reason for the change that had occurred in the process.

Later on in the day or possibly the next morning, the same thing occurred. This time I knew what it was, but still did not know why it was happening. I just basically chalked it up to a vibrational level change in me to assist Dee. I still did not know who had taken possession of my body, but I was not really concerned or frightened by it because I knew it was for the better.

Then, as I was sitting down to write this portion, Dee said to be sure to include this part in the book. I asked her why, and she said because the Angel that had taken possession of my body those two times was none other than Archangel Michael! This did not surprise me, as I had known that whoever he was, he was not there to hurt me in any way, but to help. But, Dee has been having this ongoing dialogue with Michael for some time now, especially when it comes to the Angels dealing with me. Dee is always afraid that they are taking too much out of me because sometimes the sessions get too lengthy or intense. She is very concerned for my welfare, and I thank her for that. But most of the time my body can endure what they have in store for me, and if it does get too stressful, I just quit the process and return to the here and now. This has occurred on some occasions, and they never stop me when I am at my physical limit. Dee sees and hears what they are doing to me and sometimes feels that they are doing too much at any given time and tells them to stop. Sometimes they do, but many times they just ignore her and that gets her mad. Again, I am not completely in control during these times, but when I am at my limit for a session they always honor that

CHANGES

and come to a stop before continuing at a later time. It may only be five minutes, but they do stop to let my body catch up with itself.

Today was another day in which the Angels would not leave us alone. They continued to come back again and again, sometimes with only a few minutes rest in between. Dee said she did not know what was going on, and again she hollered at them for doing so much in such a short period of time. However, during one of the sessions I saw Michael standing on the side, and I asked him what was going on and he said that it was "His Day" today. I later told this to Dee and she said that it's "His Day" everyday. I had to agree he had been quite active with us lately, and Dee reminded me that he had been with us constantly for the past couple of weeks. I had to admit, I had been seeing Michael quite a bit lately, but many times during a session I can only get a quick glimpse of people or things going on and then I forget about them afterwards. But, I remembered seeing Michael quite often lately.

51

Saturday

(11/ 5 /2005)

The Angels figured that since it was a Saturday, they could do as they pleased with us. They started out with a very intense session followed by, believe it or not, a merging session that Dee had been pleading for with them. Immediately after our very pleasurable merging session, they went directly into an extremely stressful session for a long time. After that I was completely wiped out and had to sleep for quite a while. Then, they came back for more intense sessions, each time taking more and more from my physical body. We were both pleading with them to take it easy, but it didn't work. After this I had to sleep for several hours more because I simply could not stay awake. When I finally awoke, my body felt like it was hit by a truck. I was completely drained and had no strength whatsoever. I was only awake for a short time and then had to go back to sleep again. After this second sleep I was finally able to function again.

Dee and I were complaining about her legs but the Angels also were pulling on my heart. I know that beside Michael, Raphael was there at least for the first part. Dee said later that

Raphael hung around for the entire day, but she did not say what his purpose was. I was not able to have any conversation with the Angels today because I was in a constant state of the healing process, which did not permit any outside interference.

(11/10/2005)

This morning while lying awake, but not ready to get up, I was surprised to see the Angels in a huddle of sorts talking to each other. This was something I had not seen before, and I was curious about it. I tried to go over and see what was going on, but I was not allowed to enter their circle. I said, "Fine, I guess that I am not involved with this" and left it at that. Boy was I wrong! It turned out that they were discussing what they were going to do during their next healing session with Dee and I. They had been discussing the fact that the healing session would be very hard on my body. They were thinking of taking me totally out of it so that my physical body could stand the intensity of the session.

They finally decided, fortunately for me, to take me totally out of the process from a feeling standpoint. Now this was something new to me, and I was not expecting it. They did not fill me in on their process and purpose until well into the session at a time when I was totally in their control. Fortunately, they were kind enough to explain it all to me, and I realized what they were doing was for my benefit. I could sense the session was intense, but I did not feel any of the pain. In fact, it felt like one of the easiest sessions that they had ever done with me. I was told that was their intent as I would not have been able to handle it if it had been otherwise. I was very grateful. Dee did not seem to have any ill effects from this session, and she did not feel any intense pain from it either.

Dee:

I know that there is more to this from the other day, but I do not remember it:

Babe, I'm not sure if this was the day or not, as you know they can all run together...but if it was, then it was the day that they did major work on my back, where you made me stay as long as I possibly could, and it did cause me pain to stay there. Finally, they told you if I couldn't stay any longer it was all right that I had stayed long enough for the effect to take place, but the longer I could stay, the better...so I tried my best, and then you broke the connection for me, do you remember? Or was that the time that they used our love for one another? Oh, and by the way, when you were in that age in Japan, you did talk out loud in Japanese, it was only a couple of words, but you did talk...

52

The Angels Came to Play

(11/17/2005)

The Angels came to play with a totally new feeling. As they swept in for another session, Dee felt it also and neither of us can describe this new method that they are using. It is a calm sweeping into our existence, but you know they are there. You cannot feel any real presence other than you know another presence is present within your body.

Subsequently I was taken away from the present time and taken back to a time when I was in a tropical jungle climate. I do not have a time frame or a location, other than it felt like it was thousands of years ago, a time before any city-states or organized population centers. This was definitely pre-tribal, meaning that peoples were living in small groups with very little structure to them. More like large families than anything else. I was looking through the jungle for something, and at first, I could not pick up on what it was I was looking for. Then, I started to call out a name. I cannot remember the name that I was calling, possibly due to the fact that there may not even have been a true language at that time, but never the less I was calling out for my mate. In this case it happened to be Dee; at least this is the impression that I was having. I could not find her anywhere, and I searched for her to no avail. I was comforted by the fact that I could feel Dee with me in the present since I was holding her, but it did not quiet the anxiousness or fear that I was having while trying to find her wherever I was at that time. I was told that the time frame was many thousands of years ago in the jungles of South America. I was looking for my mate, Dee, and could not find her because an animal had taken her, and I would never see her again. Although this seemed like it should be shocking to me, in the context and time frame of when it happened, it seemed like it was just a part of those times. Interestingly enough, after I had told Dee the story, she mentioned to me that the whole time during this session, she felt tremendous pain in her left foot and left side. Could this have been where the animal had attacked her?

The Angels gave us a break, for at least a whole three or four minutes before they came back again. Lately they have been coming back time after time with no regard to our ministrations of telling them that we did not want them to be coming back so often and so quickly. Like Dee said, they have been turning a cold shoulder to our requests.

I was taken back to an ancient time again, but this time I knew where I was and an approximate timeframe. I was in Japan around 1400 B.C. Once more, I was with Dee and we were a couple. I can only assume that we were privileged society because we were in our own home. We had a daughter around eight-years old, and we were having a discussion about the girl. Apparently, our daughter was to be taken to be trained in some sort of fashion that would take her away from us permanently. This seemed to be something that was done commonly in the society at that time. I do not know what kind of training, except that it had to do with the emperor. Basically, we had no choice in the matter as this was done without regard to anything the parents would want.

The interesting part of this was the child, a girl, came across to me as being Dee's son from this lifetime who happens to be an Indigo child. I guess even thousands of years ago her son was special. This is the first time that I have come across something like this, but I guess I should not be surprised. We all have lived many lifetimes and have done many different things during those lives.

Another interesting event that happened today was that the Angels decided to take advantage of us by using our love for each other. What they did is hard to explain, but we were trying to end a healing session and prevent them from starting another one when they grabbed our hearts together and began using them for their own purposes. Again, it is very difficult to explain in words, but suffice it to say that they used our hearts as a means of getting one more healing session in the time frame when we were once again trying to keep them out.

53

Starman

(11/29/2005)

I believe that we have encountered this spirit entity or one like it previously. The other day, a different entity showed up for a visit. I did not know who this was or why he was here or even why he came. The vibrational level that the entity came in with took me away. The only thing that I remember was that Dee was hollering at the Angels to stop due to the extremely high vibrational energy that they came in with, and I was completely out of touch with the situation due to that vibrational energy. I could only discern that Dee was yelling at them and saying that the level was too much for my physical body. I did not know this until Dee explained it to me later after the session.

This may have been the first time that they have put me into a situation where it overwhelmed my physical body to such an extent that my senses were completely void of any feeling at all. Dee was very upset about this. I was too when I finally understood what had happened to me. We both knew that it was Starman, as we call him, but we did not know where he had come from or why he was there. Dee finally asked his name and was told

Gastin. Neither of us is sure if he was the same entity from the past that we encountered but his energy was very similar.

When we went on to the next session we were not sure if he would be there again. So we just went with it since the Angels were not leaving us alone. They had time on their side and, of course, they used it to their advantage. But when Gastin jumped in again pushing the Angels aside, Dee became furious because of the high-energy flow that came into my body. I will try to describe it, but whatever I say will not accurately do so. I started speaking very quickly like a 33-rpm record being played at 78-rpm. This would not have been too bad, except that my entire body was undulating at this same higher frequency than normal, which is to say that my entire body eventually went into tetany, where all muscles cease to function normally. The muscles twitch until exhausted. Dee was extremely concerned and tried to bring in all the help that she could muster to have him back off me but to no avail. Eventually he let up because I could not even breathe at the time. I guess he decided that the Angels needed me around for a while longer, and killing me would not be in their best interest. I know he did not have that intention, but it was pretty intense at the time, especially when I could not do anything about it. Once he took over like that, I was completely out of it and had no conscious feelings or even knowledge of what was going on. I guess this was so that I didn't feel the discomfort or pain that it caused my body to undergo. Again, I am completely confident that he intended me no harm in any way by doing this. I just think that since he was not in the physical, he forgot that my physical body could only withstand so much at any given time. That's one reason why both Dee and I get upset with the Angels from time to time because they run sessions too close together, with no time for my physical body to recuperate.

However, the Angels are generally pretty good about the pain. Pain, most of the time, just passes through me without my body really feeling it too much. Sometimes, as in the past day or so with Gastin, I had to tell him to stop due to the intense feelings that I was experiencing. Mostly the Angels listen and take the pain away. But I had to make a deal yesterday with them, so that I could continue. I was feeling a lot of pain; usually this occurs in my heart when they go really deep down into my heart at some of the deepest levels imaginable. But when I asked them to take the pain away, they ignored me. I called in Archangel Michael and Archangel Raphael, who have been with us recently, and asked that they help to stop this pain that I was feeling. Neither of them could do anything about it, and the pain was getting more intense.

With this intense pain continuing with no sign of relief, and with no end of the session in site, I was getting desperate to do something because I was about at the end of my rope. Then, I got the thought of making a deal with Gastin. I told him to take the pain away, and he could continue with the session for as long as was needed. I thanked the Angels for helping Dee with these healings, and I told them that they could continue as long as I was relieved of the pain. As soon as I had told him this, the pain ceased. The session then went on for a good amount of time, but I was relatively pain free for the duration. Dee also experienced pain during these sessions, but fortunately in most cases her pain is not as intense as it is on my body. However, she gets quite tired after many of these healings.

Today I was being pulled in my heart and by my arm to start another session with the Angels. I knew that Gastin was still around. I could *feel* him. We decided to go ahead, but we were prepared for what was to come.

As soon as they started, they began to tease me by just working on my heart and some lower vibrational energies. I knew what was going on, so I told them to stop fooling around because I knew that Gastin was there just waiting to jump in and get started at the higher vibrational levels. No sooner did I say that, Gastin jumped in with his much higher frequencies, which just tore up my body. There were two somewhat long and very high vibrational adjustments, and then I was given a few seconds rest. I knew that I was deliberately being given this few seconds rest, and I told Dee to get ready for one more which I knew would be a hum dinger. It was. It started off like the previous ones, but it continued on for a longer duration and, as it continued, the vibrational level began to rise. This continued for probably just a couple of minutes, but when you are in this turmoil it feels like forever. I was to a point where I thought that I would pass out if they continued any further which I was able to pass on to Gastin by my thoughts, and I guess he took pity on me because as soon as I had thought about it, he let go. I was completely and utterly wiped out by this. I began to breathe very quickly and very deeply. My body felt completely disconnected from me, and I could not move my legs or arms. I asked Dee to just caress my body so that I knew I was still here and had not passed over or through the veil.

I was in this condition for about a half an hour before I was able to move about again. I knew that session would be intense, but I was not really prepared for something like what had just occurred. I have no long-term ill effects from these types of occurrences, and I do know that anything that happens during these sessions cannot hurt me in any way. I completely believe that, or I would not be doing these sessions in the first place. Besides, how could anything happen when I've got all of my Angels around me?

I realized after the session that during the session with Gastin, he had taken me out of the feeling part of it by taking me on an adventure. I was flying through space and I felt I was traveling toward his planet. I was able to see all around us that space is mostly just that --empty space with nothing around. I could see galaxies off in any direction, but they were all very far away and small. It seemed like we were just cruising along at a comfortable speed in space. We never reached his planet because by this time my body was ready to shut down, and I had to end the session. I did not even recall this traveling with Gastin until about fifteen minutes after the session stopped.

Mega was in the peanut gallery yesterday during a session, and I could feel that he was just waiting for his turn at bat (meaning his time to have fun with me during a session). Since we were already into a session he got up for his turn, and did he ever enjoy himself! Of course, it was at my expense. He started to work on Dee's back that coincided with some feelings and a little pain in my back. But as he was getting into it, I could tell, as could

Dee, that he was really enjoying his work. I guess he figured that he had to get his licks in while he had the opportunity. His session was totally on my back but he just kept on going and going (like the Energizer Bunny), the only difference is that this was my back and Dee's that he was dealing with. Since the pain was not too bad, and we knew that what he was doing was a good thing, both Dee and I just let him continue until he got his fill. Eventually, the session ended with no harm done to either of us and at least Mega was able to get his turn in also. We thanked him for his help, and he went back into the lineup with the others until needed again.

(12/3/2005)

As a new day arrived, the Angels were there waiting for us to begin again. We started out in the usual way but then all of a sudden, Gastin jumped into the fray. Dee had spoken to him to tell him that if he was going to be there to work on me, he had to lower his vibrational level so my body could absorb it without being so tortured. Dee said she was told, "But he is from the Root Race, he is family". Dee told him she knows that I am family, but Gastin still had to go slowly because my physical body could not stand the higher vibrational levels he had been using. Dee thought that Gastin understood what she was talking about, especially when he first jumped in to the session, but he very quickly ramped up the energy to a much higher frequency. This, Dee did not like at all, and she told him so. She began to tell him to stop but, of course, she was ignored at first. However, with her persistence he did finally lower the vibrations to a tolerable degree.

At the end of the session Gastin actually stepped into and spoke through me. I sat up with the frequency of the vibrations, and Dee held on to me. She laid me back down, and then Gastin quietly left, this time my body was able to return to normal in a much easier transition than the last time. Neither of us knew that Gastin was able to do this. After the bout with Gastin, the Angels wanted to continue with another session, but we felt as though we had had enough for the time being, so Dee got up. Not two minutes went by and they were back again, this time it was Michael, and he promised that it would only be another half an hour, and it would only be very smooth and nothing intense at all. He kept to his promise.

Dee reminded me of something that I forgot. This had only happened in the past couple of days. The Angels began to sing to Dee during the session that she thinks is pretty cool. I had only a vague recollection of them singing during these times, and I do not know how well they sing. I don't know what could have given them the idea to start singing, but we are enjoying this newfound connection with the Angels.

This morning the Angels told me they would be around all day, and they have been. Gastin came back also. He just jumped in without my having any previous knowledge that he was coming. I felt him coming with about three seconds notice and then he was there at his typical accelerated rate. Dee knew that he was around but, for some reason, I cannot feel his presence until he hits me. I think it's possible that I don't feel him because he does not want me to. Not that he is a danger or anything, but I guess if

I knew he was coming, my body might react differently or put up some kind of defense to keep him at bay. This is just speculation on my part.

In regard to Gastin though, it occurred to me this afternoon that his being here is entirely for me and not for Dee. He was helping me to get to a higher vibrational level, one that Dee is already beyond. I said to her, "How high are you anyway?", and she replied that she didn't know. Not that it matters. I have come so far and my vibrations have been raised so much that to realize that Dee is still ahead of me is just a profound thought. But then again, I started from scratch, and she has been there all of this lifetime. I guess not being up to her level yet is not such a bad thing. Besides, I still cannot have direct conversations with the Angels like she does on a daily basis. I just find that fact alone so fascinating, and it is one that Dee doesn't take for granted, but she does forget sometimes that the rest of us still have a long distance to go in order to be able to do what she does at will.

During this afternoon session with the Angels in which we were continually brought from here to there for a few hours, I suddenly was pulled from somewhere in the Ether to do a retrieval. Now I have done retrievals in the past (as you are aware) but this was the first time that I was being pulled towards doing one while in a healing session. I told this to Dee, and she said we usually do them while we are asleep and many times we don't remember them, so I'm sure that we do them on a continual basis. But, this was a different feeling, one that I was experiencing in my physical body, and it needed to be addressed. Therefore, I tried to go to Focus 23 to find someone who needed help. But since we had been doing healing sessions all afternoon, I found that my mind would not take me to Focus 23. After several unsuccessful attempts, I decided that Dee was right, and I would do the retrieval while asleep tonight.

While just relaxing after a session, I was very softly and gently pulled into the Angel's realm again. They have done this the past couple of days where I just gently glide into their arms with no forewarning or different feeling. The only way I know that it has occurred is that I suddenly realize that my breathing has increased, and they generally start to speak Angelic to me. When I finally realized that they had taken me again, I just figured it was for another session with them, and I went along with it. That feeling did not last long. I was suddenly aware of an Indian woman with an infant. Dee said that I was speaking in an Indian dialect or singing in one anyway, and there were others around although I do not recall who they were. They may have been with the woman, but I am not sure.

As time went on, I saw this woman and her child falling into an endless cavern. I was carried along with them. Once we stopped falling, we were alone. I mean, the woman and I were alone! Her child was gone, and I instinctively realized what had occurred. She had died with her child and now she was searching for the baby. I could feel her panic and despair. This had happened very quickly. She came running over to me, being as I was the only other one there, and started screaming about her baby being lost. I tried to calm her down but she went running off, searching for her child. I felt helpless watching this unfold. Eventually she came back to me and was exhausted as well as distraught. This time I was able to calm her down and get her to listen to me. Instead of telling her that she was dead and that she and her baby were okay, I decided the best method would be just to take her to her child. I told her that I could take her to where her child was, and she calmed down a bit more and was anxious for me to take her there. I grasped her hand and started walking to the Park. Sure enough there was her child being held in the arms of someone she knew. She just took off and went directly to her child. This was the end of the retrieval, and I was soon brought back.

54

A Journey of Light

(1/19/2006)

The other day while working with the Angels Dee and I were taken on a journey of light. Both of us were emanating some form of light energy – mine was a deep maroon color and Dee's was a golden color. When we eventually merged our two colors together an amazing thing happened, the two colors were changed into one very bright and intense royal blue! It was a very beautiful royal blue tending towards the violet in the most spiritual way imaginable. For these types of moment's words only pale; suffice it to say, that moment was truly breathtaking.

We had been told there would be a change in the New Year. When the Angels came today they started a new phase of this journey for us. While we were holding each other and our hearts had merged together; there was a new kind of feeling. The only way that I can try to describe that feeling is that if you fill up a bathtub with warm water and spread your fingers out, and run your fingers through the surface of the water. Feeling the water rushing through your fingers, you experience a tingling along the sides of your fingers. Now, you have some vague idea of what I am talking about. You have to multiply that feeling ten fold and feel it in every cell of your fingers while it tingles up through your hand and arm and reaches all the way to the back of your neck and down your spine. This is the best description that I can come up with.

I was about to tell the Angels to stop because I could not go on with this feeling any longer, when all of a sudden Dee said, "I love you." Now, she did not have any idea that I was about to tell the Angels to stop due to the feelings that I was having, but as soon as she said I love you, the vibrational tone that I was feeling completely changed. We were still merged on the soul level, but either my level of vibration changed to one of being more acceptable, or I was brought up to a new level, one more compatible to the one Dee was on, so there was an evenness to our levels.

While this was a totally new feeling that I experienced, I was also able to figure out that this was a new area for us. I could feel that whatever the Angels were doing was at the cellular level. This was an area I had not felt before. I could actually feel something changing as I was holding Dee close to me. Hopefully, this new feeling and new area of work are the changes we were told about before the New Year. For my part I had been a bit antsy lately because I wanted Dee to get well so badly and when that went on for awhile without any real gains, I blamed myself for not trying hard enough or not doing exactly what I should be doing for her. I knew that I should not feel lacking in this area, but I did. I could see how far she had come over the past several months, but I wanted to see continual improvement on a constant basis. However, this did not happen. Improvements came incrementally over time.

We were on a new track now and one that will bring forth definitive results in the not too distant future. Either way, we will continue with this work since we both know that this is the right path for us.

Dee:

Rich is right in that I didn't know at the time what was transpiring in him, but he had interpreted correctly that my vibration was working along with the Angels to shift his; so, on a much deeper level, I knew what to do. Another thing that has to be understood is Rich is not lacking in any way where my healing is concerned. There had always been a reason or purpose for everything, and a time for me to be healed completely. I have faith that I will be without pain when the time is right. We are working towards that goal together, as one, along with the best of the best you could ever ask for. Along the way, we are experiencing the most joyous of journeys of the spirit realm, of Divine Love, and so much more.

55

Raising My Level

(1/30/2006)

The only thing that has changed this month has been the deepness of merging that the Angels have been doing with us. These sessions are now usually longer than they had been, sometimes lasting around forty minutes, but usually twenty to thirty minutes. The effect that we have noticed is that when they are finished with a session, both Dee and I quickly fall into a deep sleep for anywhere from half an hour to one hour in duration. We both feel the Angels are continuing their work during these periods, but neither of us can remember what they were during this time. I usually fall into a deep sleep and often Dee awakens before I do, and she gets up while I am still sound asleep. This has been happening quite often now, and we hoped to see greater results from it.

Dee:

I have found that during these sessions the Angels seemed to be working mostly on continuing to raise Rich's vibrational level, along with doing work on DNA/RNA. Every once in a while they did healing work, but for the most part at this time they were working to bring Rich's vibrational level up to my own, so that we may then shift together. Since the beginning of our sessions with the Angels they had always called me Anya (through Rich of course). In subsequent sessions, I found out the reason. Anya was my original name. So, in one of the sessions, I had asked the Angels if they could tell me what Rich's original name was. They told me it was Abrahma. Through these sessions we had been able to experience many past life events, and although I don't feel as though we had actually seen who we were as Anya and Abrahma, "we knew" who we were, so to speak. These sessions left us very tired and wiped out, especially Rich. I am not surprised because he was the one going through all of the vibrational shifting.

(2/05/2006)

Last night I felt the presence of Archangel Michael come in about half way through the session. I said this to Dee and she immediately said that she was talking to him at that same time. This morning during a session I again felt the presence of Michael, and I again said this to Dee and again she said that she had just been talking to him. I made a point to myself to remember these two incidents and to tell Dee about them later on. When we were having coffee Dee said, "What a wonderful confirmation it was that at those two times when I had been talking to Michael, you felt his presence and were able to tell me so." This was going to be the exact same thing that I was going to tell her about the sessions too! It is just such a beautiful experience to be as connected as the two of us are.

Dee:

RAISING MY LEVEL

I had been missing Archangel Michael's presence during our sessions, so as Rich and I connected I called out to him in my mind. In no time, he was right there. I asked him where he had been, because I hadn't felt his presence around, nor did Rich or he would have said something. He said that he was always around if we needed him (of course!). To my surprise though, I hadn't told Rich I was going to do this, and during the session he said "Michael." It was during the time that I was still speaking to Michael. That totally blew my mind, because it confirmed our connection even more. Not only that, but the next morning Michael showed up again, and I was speaking to him, and once again Rich said his name. Many times during our sessions we had confirmed, or put together my sight and his feelings, just which Angel or Angels were present, but this time was most definitely wonderful.

(2/11/2006)

Last night during a session with the Angels I knew that Michael and Raphael were both there, and I remember telling Dee "two" referring to both of them at the time. I think she understood because when we are in a session with the Angels I cannot always communicate what I am experiencing completely to her due to the fact that I am bilocated during the sessions. Many times I can get in a word or two or more but whole sentences during these periods are rare. Usually Dee can pick up what I am referring to because she is usually "seeing" what I perceive.

I felt Michael delving directly into my heart and Dee mentioned that she felt him in her heart at the same time, indicating that we were on the same wavelength. When I mentioned 'Two" she said, "Uh-huh", indicating that she knew that more than one Angel was there. I think afterwards Dee said that she saw someone else there, but I don't recall if she said it was Raphael or not. She will have to add her thoughts and impressions to fill in those details. The interesting part was when Michael was touching my heart; he was also working on Dee's heart at the same time. We can literally feel the same thing at the same time. We felt Michael's hand moving back and forth between our two bodies, working and moving our DNA/RNA around. It is quite an intense feeling when this happens, and it is difficult for me to let it go on for too long before I have to ask him to stop and come back later. Then, I fall into a deep sleep quickly.

Dee:

During last nights session I was just about to tell Rich that Raphael was also present when he said the word "two". It was totally unbelievable to me, but then again not; it seems as though our connection is deepening, if that is possible. Which brings me to a thought that just crossed my mind; Michael had told me that one part of the process was to deepen our connection. I had said to him at that time, "Is it possible for it to get any deeper than it already is?" He informed me, that it was very possible to get much deeper, and I had forgotten about it until this moment. While Michael had his hand in between both of our hearts I have to say it was most uncomfortable -- not painful --. but strange, it is almost like a heavy prodding and, of course, is something so new. I can tell you that Rich was making the same exact sounds at the same time as I was, so I know he was feeling the same type of sensations.

56

A Trip Back to the Ether

(2/12/2006)

Today I did something that I have not done for a long time; I took a trip to the Ether. It had been quite some time since I accessed Focus 23 through Focus 27, but I decided to give it a try to see what would happen. Most of the experience was just a compilation of wonderful feelings that one experiences while passing through the different Focus levels. When I passed through Focus 23 I consciously looked around for anyone who might need my help but found no one. I continued on, and ended up in Focus 27 that is such a wonderful place to be. The sun is always shinning, the Park and the site are so beautiful to experience that I usually just want to stay there and never return to the physical world. However, we are still in the physical so ultimately we must return to the body and continue our existence. When I was getting near my time to return, all of a sudden I found myself in a battlefield medical unit with a nurse calling to me that she needed my help with a patient. I naturally went to assist her without fully comprehending what was happening. Then, it dawned on me that she needed to be moved on to the light. I had to figure out a way to get her to realize that these people no longer needed her. It was her turn to move on, like she had helped so many do during her time.

I am not sure which war this was, perhaps the Korean War in the early 1950's, but it really does not matter. I was there to help her realize she should move on and that's all that counted. She helped a patient and then quickly went to the next in her triage. I went over to her with the patient that she was assisting and quietly said to her that she had helped these people enough, and it was time for her to go. She didn't quite understand, although I felt that she had a sense of relief when I told her. She said there were still many who needed help and she could not leave at this time. I told her it was okay for her to leave because she, along with the other men injured there, were past the time for healing on the Earth Plane. She seemed to understand intuitively what I was saying, possibly because she remembered the mortar round coming into the field hospital earlier. She accepted the fact that she had done all she could, and asked, "What do I do now?" I told her that I could bring her to a place where she would be reunited with loved ones, and she accepted that. So, we started to walk along and very quickly she exclaimed "Bob and Tom!" These were both soldiers that I assumed had been in her care, and passed over, because they were young men looking very fit in their battle uniforms. She shed tears of joy when she was reunited with them. They just continued to walk along the path and quickly disappeared. I was very glad to see that, and as I was no longer needed, I decided to come back; knowing that I had helped another soul, in a very small way, to continue their journey into the light.

57

Light and Darkness

(2/25/2006)

The last twenty-four hours have been a real roller coaster ride -- light and dark, good and evil, and choosing right from wrong, has been the theme throughout. The Angels started by not leaving us alone for any long period of time. Anytime we would finish with them, they just pulled us back in before we could stop them. After every session I would just pass right out for an hour or so. I would not even be able to get out of bed. Dee was not as affected as she was able to get up after a period of time, but I was more or less stuck with absolutely no strength to move at all. During the few occasions when I was able to eventually drag myself out of bed, it was only for a short period of time because they would be right there again pulling me back. If I disregarded them, they would start to pull on Dee along with me. We simply did not have much of a choice in the matter.

We were taken to many different locales during these sessions. I was taken back by falling in time, which is a very upsetting thing because you really feel as if you are falling through space. I have somewhat become accustomed to this due to the fact that Dee is always there with me and reassuring me that I am not really falling physically but only mentally. This makes the sensation much easier for my mind to understand since, if you realize that someone is holding you in the physical, you need not worry about getting injured. I remembered one time telling Dee," Stay with me, stay with me." I don't know why I was saying this, but Dee told me she was always with me, and I felt much better. There was another time when I was very distraught and began to cry uncontrollably for a long time, and Dee kept asking, "What is wrong?" When I was able to gain enough composure to speak, all I could say was that they were all dead. Dee kept prompting me for more information, and it began to emerge that I was on an ancient battlefield and there were many dead soldiers there after a major battle. Dee continued to try to get more information from me about when and where it had taken place, but due to my condition at the time, the only thing I could say was "Rome." I can only think this was a situation that I had not confronted before in one of my past lives and, therefore, was not able to deal with it on a one-time basis.

Other instances began to make sense to me when Dee put it in the perspective of good vs. evil. Looking back at some of the things I remembered, I got the feeling of light and darkness. Unfortunately, these things occurred over a long period of time, and it is possible that my mind just could not process them all.

(2/26/2006)

Last night was another eventful evening as the Angel Johanas took me back to the time of the previous session. I fought this off due to the extreme emotions that I had experienced during that timeframe. I was successful in not going back the first time, but during a subsequent session I succumbed to his wishes, partly due to the fact that I knew it was better for me to go there, experience what I needed, and then I would be able to move on from there. In the meantime I knew that if I did not go I would be stuck and not have any further lessons. So I went. I was extremely fearful of what was going to happen and as it turned out, rightfully so. Apparently I had been in charge of a Legion of approximately one thousand soldiers for this battle. It was during the earlier part of the Roman Empire, even before they were referred to as an empire, approximately three thousand years ago, as far as I could tell from the impressions I was receiving.

We had been in several previous skirmishes with this enemy and had survived quite nicely. Now was the time for a bigger engagement. I felt I was given a choice of attacking from the East or the South. I chose the East after surveying the battlefield and our enemy's defenses. As it turned out, I chose wrong. We were met with attacks from the North and West. We had been lured into an area where the terrain was deceiving and allowed our enemy to hide quite well. They were able to get around and out flank us. It was a disastrous battle. We were annihilated from all sides, much the same way Napoleon was beaten at Waterloo. The result was the loss of almost my entire column. The slaughter was entirely my fault, and I was made to pay the price.

The price during these times was a steep one indeed. I was summarily executed with one stab of a sword in my left side. A curious thing happened right after I had seen this whole scene played out. I immediately felt a terrific pain in my left side between the ribs. Immediately I knew this was the pain from the sword that I had experienced so many thousands of years ago. It was so real and so painful that I had to ask Dee to use her healing energy on the location to ease the pain, and it helped.

After analyzing what had happened, it occurred to me that what Johanas had said to Dee earlier was really what all of this was about. He told her there was some unfinished business that I needed to attend to. I was carrying this guilt around with me for three thousand years, and it was time to confront it, to face it head on, see if there was any alternative to my actions, and see how things played out. No matter if I had chosen to attack from the East or the South, I firmly believe the results would have been the same. We were outnumbered and there was no way out. The men would have died either way. I had to come to realize that the outcome would have been the same. That may take a little time on my part. Knowing that something may be out of my control, and coming to terms with it, is not easy. You have to forgive yourself and release it!

Madagascar told me today that these types of sessions would only continue until we go to Sedona on Tuesday. She said they have something new for us when we get there.

Dee:

I have to say that the Angels were really doing a job on us. Well, mostly on Rich, as he takes the brunt of it. I kept on asking Johanas what was going on, and at first I honestly didn't understand what he was trying to tell me. Sometimes they can be pretty cryptic. I couldn't grasp what darkness against the light that Rich was fighting or had to fight. He then said something like "releasing". When I told him I wasn't sure of what he meant, he told me it was a cleansing of sorts. They have also been working on shifting Rich's vibration and activating his DNA/RNA. I had asked Johanas if this would be the last for him, and was told yes and no. He told me what they were doing at this time was very important to help Rich, so that his vibration will be elevated enough to ascend to the higher realms or dimensions. After that, we will both shift together. As for Rich's experience in the Rome battlefield, I do believe he has remembered it all correctly. As the only thing he told me the first time was "they're all dead" and "my fault". When I asked him," Who was dead?" He responded with "My men, all dead". I then asked him where he was, and he told me Rome. Then, I tried to explain to him, that it wasn't his fault, and at that time, he wouldn't have any of it. It wasn't until he went back, and witnessed everything, or I should say, lived through everything that he came to the realization that he had been carrying around all of this guilt.

58

Twin Flames

Twin Flames are two bodies with one soul! Dee and I are definitely Twin Flames. If you are interested in this topic, you can read about the concept in *Twin Souls – Finding Your True Spiritual Partner* by Dr. Maury Pressman and Patricia Joudry.

Learning about your Twin Flame is like finding your Yin for your Yang. It is said that Creator took one soul and divided its essence into two equal parts, (like identical Twins who are equal but opposite in order to experience the totality of existence.) Each time we incarnate into the physical I believe the emptiness we feel, is that lack of our other half. We may not get to meet our Twin Flame in every lifetime that we experience, but when you do you know the difference, believe me. It is like being with someone where both of your hearts and souls are "One". Now, Twin Flames are reuniting all over to restore the order and unity of God's creations and to disintegrate the consciousness of this duality.

Humanity today is on the brink of a quantum leap in

the advancement of consciousness. There are more enlightened people than ever before realizing that now is the time to reawaken ourselves to our origins, and the responsibilities that we have towards ourselves, and the Earth.

59

Sedona II

(3/6/2006)

When we returned to Sedona we were excited and looking forward to some special times. The Angels told us that things would change in Sedona and they certainly have.

We went to Cathedral Rock on the riverbank side by Red Creek since we did not go the last time we were here. We were told that it was worth the trip because you get a totally different view of the red rock formations from the riverside. We were looking forward to it. We arrived at a good time; the river was low due to a drought that they were experiencing, which allowed you to cross the river without getting wet. There is no bridge to cross. If the river is running high, you cannot get to the other side so that you can get closer to Cathedral Rock. The river basin is wide and flat with many volcanic rocks having been washed downstream over the centuries with flat plateau areas where the red rock is just magnificent. We ventured over, and sat down by the river on the rocks and enjoyed the peaceful tranquility and the power that you feel just by being there. After a few minutes of soaking up the energy, I closed my eyes for an instant. As soon as they were closed, I saw a great battle between two Indian tribes trans-piring right in the area where we were sitting. This jolted me, and I told Dee about what had just happened.

After a few more minutes I again closed my eyes, and I saw four horses walking gently up the stream just off to our side. One was an Appaloosa and the others were just one color. Dee then asked me if I saw the Indians that were riding atop the horses. I said, "No, I only saw them from the bottom half and only their legs were visible to me." I did not realize it at the time, but there was a reason that I could only see them from that perspective. A short time later after sitting quietly again with my eyes closed, I saw a little Indian girl no more than five-years old by the river. She was running to tell her mother that there were horses and men coming up the river. I then realized that I was this little girl, and from her perspective she could not see higher than the bottom half of the horses. That is why I could not tell what the Indians looked like when Dee had asked me. My mother went on to explain to me that I did not have to be afraid of these men because they were here to trade goods with our tribe. This was all that I was able to see from that time frame, but it was a most enjoyable experience.

Later on during our journey around Sedona, we went back to Montezuma's Well, because that area had struck me with such tremendous energy the last time we were there. The most intense energy was at the ruins of a pit house that is located at the well site. It is an area that many people just drive by and do not pay much attention to since it is really only a hole in the ground with some areas dug out to show where the Indians would have put poles up to support a roof. But this is an area of extremely powerful energy, and we had to revisit it this time around to feel what we could experience. I could feel the energy of the site as soon as I stepped from the car on arrival. We had wanted to experience this area without others around, and we were granted some time there alone, free from other visitors. I just had to sit down on the ground by the pit house and experience the raw energy of the place. I must have been there for about twenty minutes with Dee. She was taking pictures of the site, and I was quietly meditating.

When we were ready to go, Dee asked if I had gotten any information on the people who had lived there -- the Sinagua Indians. They grew crops without water at least that is what the archaeologists say. But I was not getting any information about the tribe or anything else for that matter during that time. I was only experiencing a deep feeling of gratitude and thankfulness for being able to be there with Dee and absorbing as much of the energy around as possible. This was quite a trip because the energy in this area can make you dizzy due to the power associated with this site. We thanked spirit for allowing us to experience this, and we moved on to the well, which was beautiful and full of energy.

(3/8/2006)

Dee was telling me about Emanuel who had come to us only in Sedona. His energy was very strong, and I could only take it for a certain amount of time before I was totally drained. I also had to go right to sleep afterwards because I was so tired. It's a good thing he usually came at night (when I was supposed to rest anyway) so I did not miss any of the days there. Dee explained to me that Emanuel was another name for Yeshuah when He was born, and it dawned on me that I had seen a very clear face of the Christ the night before. It was only for an instant, but I had clearly seen him. All of the energy in Sedona had seemed to throw off our usual ability to remember and understand what goes on during our sessions. Most of what either of us could remember was just glimpses or disjointed portions of what had been going on.

During a late morning session with the Angels, Emanuel said that He was coming to us in Sedona at a much higher level than normally due to the higher energy that is surrounding the whole area. He did not say it, but the impression I received was that here in Sedona He was referred to as Emanuel instead of Yeshuah or Christ. While Sedona was beautiful and had wonderful energy, Dee and I did not find an area in, or surrounding that resonated with us in order to buy a home there.

60

The Triple Crown

(3/18/2006)

There have been three Angels working together with us this month since our return from Sedona. We still do not know who they are as neither Michael nor Madagascar will fill us in. Dee has named them the Triple Crown. We can tell which one is working on us as they each have a different energy signature. One of them is very strong when he works on our hearts. Another works strictly with our legs, as I have been immobilized from the waist down several times as he does his work, and sometimes, for almost an hour afterwards. This is not a comfortable feeling. When you are immobilized you tend to get a bit anxious because you do not have control of your body. Knowing who is doing this makes it a bit easier to take. The third Angel's work is a much gentler type of energy. He works mainly with our heart energy, but it is not as intense as the other energies that we experienced. One of the side effects of these Angel's work is that we both get extremely tired after they have a session with us and we need to sleep sometimes for almost two hours afterwards. That is why we make sure that we have the time to devote to them.

Dee:

Actually, when these three Angels first came in the impression I received was "Triple Crown". It was not just something I decided to name them. As they weren't individually giving information of themselves at that time, the only impression given was the one I received. Of course, asking the other Angels wasn't any help, as it always seems they expect us to do our work for ourselves.

(3/26/2006-A)

We finally know a bit more about the three Angels working with us, but I'll let Dee fill you in on those details. The energy from one of the three Angels is entirely different from the others. Thus, it easy to know who is working on us, but several times there has been another energy sneaking in occasionally to help us out. We are very familiar with this energy, it is Michael's. His energy is well known to us and easily identifiable, even when he occasionally comes into a session already in progress. He did this to us this morning. The three were working with us and all of a sudden there was a noticeable change in energy vibration. Dee said, "I know, Michael". He had come to work on my heart for recalibration. During this time I was feeling a very strong hold on my heart. This process kept up for quite sometime. The intenseness of the session and having multiple sessions during the night exhausted us both. We requested a break from Michael and told him he could continue at another time. He was kind enough to let us go at that moment so we could relax, but he came back within a couple of minutes to some strong energy again. Neither of us was prepared for this, and we had to tell Michael again that "later" in our frame of reference was not two minutes from before. We are constantly fighting with them about this time thing, which they just cannot understand. Our linear time frame is just too foreign a concept for them to "get". We keep trying, knowing that they mean no harm, it's just they have no reference point from which to gauge these things.

We do know that the three of these new angels are here to work as a team with us and that they can work at the same time. This presents some difficulty for us as their energy systems overlap, which causes our bodies to respond in strange ways. The other day as they were working on both of our hearts and legs at the same time, I was ultimately so stuck that my legs would literally not move for almost an hour. I had to have Dee physically remove my legs from being in contact with hers and my body was stuck from the waist down. Dee's legs were in tremendous pain at this time, and I wanted to do healing energy on them for her, but I could not get out of bed. So I rolled off the bed and literally dragged my body to the couch with her help so that I could get in a position to help her release the pain in her legs. Having leg pain or some other residual pain after a session is not that uncommon, but one of us can usually help the other. However, with this new energy they are using, it took its toll on both of us at the same time, and made it very difficult to help each other.

The intense Chinese energy that I had experienced months ago came back with a vengeance. This time I was taken back to the time frame of Genghis Khan in the early 1200's. I saw that I was a warrior in his army. I was an officer in command of several regiments. I enjoyed the battles and the killing and pillaging and the murder of innocent women and children. It was just as easy to do as the killing of an enemy soldier. This was somewhat hard for my psyche to understand, as I have never seen myself as an evil person in any of my previous incarnations. This did not sit well with me, even though I had known intuitively that sometime in my past I must have been this type of a person.

These incidents were marked by a very different physical experience during our sessions. Dee was concerned for me because she said that my breathing became very shallow and my body was in a state of tetany. I recall that I would feel my physical body being pushed down deeply into the bed. It was as if my physical body had dropped miles into the bed, and I recall a feeling of being paralyzed during those times. I cannot remember any more of the physical aspects, but they were very extreme in nature.

All of this information took several trips back to fully unfold. I saw that originally I was not part of Khan's army but had belonged to a village that had been overrun by his army. At the time I was given a choice of joining his army or being killed. I chose life. It was not uncommon for the locals to join up with the conquering army. This is the way that the army itself increased. I did notice that up to this point in time, I was not a very ferocious warrior, just someone who did what he had to do to protect his village. But all of that changed when the army of Khan came to town. They had murdered most of the civilians and took the spoils for themselves. This vile warfare was abhorrent at first until I was exposed to the other side of it as a warrior. Soon I participated in the same violence and cruelty as the other warriors and enjoyed it. This is not a part of my past that I am extremely proud of, but those were different times with different rules.

After quite a bit of thinking about those times, I have determined that because of the extreme acts of cruelty that I had performed, and the fact that it is so abhorrent to me today, the strong mental reactions that I experience whenever this past life is conjured up, were responsible for the intense physical reactions. Dee told me that I had to confront this and it made sense to me. Now, having confronted this part of my past, and forgiving myself and releasing my weaknesses and guilt, I feel that I can move on.

Dee:

The three Angels (in order) are Vincent; he is the first Angel of the Triple Crown, and works on the heart in a very intense manner with his energies. When he comes in, Rich always warns me, "it's #1 or, now that he knows his name, he will sometimes say, "Vincent". The second Angel's name is Aragon. He works on the legs and his energies are subtler. The third Angel is Mercada, or Mercado, and his energies are to me, a combination of the other two. He doesn't seem to come very often. They tend to show themselves to me wearing hooded cloaks, but I know the difference between them as Vincent has Black hair, Aragon has blonde, and Mercado curly brown.

As for Rich's experience's with the past life in Genghis Khan's army, I never told him, but from the beginning I knew that was where this experience was from. I had seen the army on their horses many times, whenever he was thrown into that experience. I was told the energy of that particular lifetime did not serve him. It has taken a very long time for it to come forward, but everything comes as it is supposed to. In the last few sessions where Rich really found out the nature of this experience and lifetime, his whole body would go stiff, and his breathing would get really shallow. It wasn't like he was sleeping at all, because he was not limp. It was only after a long period of time that he would either start to whimper, or say a few mumbling words, and his body would release.

(3/26/2006-B)

This afternoon we were called by the Angels for a session and while lying down in one of our normal positions waiting for the Angels to appear nothing happened. This occasionally does happen, but this time the Angels had been bothering us terribly to have a session. They bother us by either making Dee feel very dizzy or taking my left arm and shaking it several times. I know this may sound odd, but I assure you that this occurs to us on a daily basis. At first we did not know what to make of it, but now that we have been experiencing these things for the better part of a year, they have become commonplace to us. At least the nudging part of these experiences is commonplace, but the rest of it, particularly the experiences themselves during the sessions, are completely new mostly each and every time we lie down to have one.

As we were lying down and expecting them to start, they were still shaking my left arm, which does happen sometimes before they start. This time was a bit different, as the period of time seemed to go on for longer than normal. I asked them, "What was happening?" They responded, "Tell Dee to lie on her back as we are going to work on her right arm." I said to Dee, "Lie on your back", and sure enough, as soon as she turned over they started. This is just another example of how they just do not comprehend the physical from the spirit world. Timeframes mean nothing as everything happens at one time for them. I did not recognize the energy patterns of the entity working on us and told this to Dee. She said she had asked, and was told something, but I do not recall what it was. It was different from other energy patterns that we had previously experienced. It is quite interesting that we can tell who is coming through to us just by the energy they display. They each have a signature pattern.

During this particular session I found that I had to move my right leg over Dee's right leg. As soon as I had done this, Dee said she felt a sharp pain in her right foot. Then, I felt energy from the Angels running through the entire right side of her body. This went on for sometime. When they finally released us from this session, we were both a bit tired, so we just relaxed for a few minutes. They told me they were coming back for more. However, this time we had to be in our normal position of me on my back and Dee on her stomach with her arm over me.

When the three Angels jumped in we immediately knew who they were because one started at my heart very quickly and harshly, and number three went right for our legs. This is their normal process. After a while they may switch as they proceed. This time was different. During the "quiet" time of one of them changing off to the other, I felt someone stick their finger in between my ribs into my heart. This was an odd feeling, uncomfortable but not painful. I did not really recognize the energy signature, and no Angel had previously done this quite the same way. I was at a loss to know who it was, although I did have an idea of the entity. This went on for a bit of time and I said to Dee, "Is Raphael here?" and she said, "Yes." I replied, "He is pushing his fingers into my ribs, which is not a common way for him to approach me." I felt it was him from the start but his approach was different, and I could not latch onto the energy because it felt different, yet familiar. I was not completely sure who it was. When Dee confirmed it was him for me, he then immediately went to my heart and began his work.

When he finally got down to business, Dee fell asleep. The Angels started to sing to Dee during this time, and I realized that one of the reasons that they sing is to take her mind and my mind off what is happening to us physically. Especially when Michael is around, because of the intense feelings we experience are somewhat painful, and the singing by the Angels distracts us from the pain.

Dee:

Raphael made a surprise visit today, along with Michael. We knew the energy coming in was a bit different as Raphael hadn't been around for a while; it was nice to see him and feel his energy once more. Normally Raphael just gives me a profile of himself, but this time he showed himself close up and almost full body! What I saw was actually different from what I expected him to look like. When he had always shown himself to me previously I had always thought of him with darker features, not real dark mind you, but nevertheless dark. He had the brightest blue eyes I had ever seen, and his hair was a lighter shade than I thought, although it still had a curl to it, but flatter near the top, almost like a shag haircut.

61

Michael and My Heart

(3/28/2006)

Today, an astonishing event happened to us! During a session, Archangel Michael came in and began to work on my heart. This in itself was not unusual because he comes quite frequently to help us, but today when he came in, the session began to get very intense. At first the feelings were "normal" for Michael but then all of a sudden, Michael literally grabbed my heart with his two hands! I could feel his fingers wrapped around my heart and he was doing some type of manipulation with his fingers. I could not believe what I was feeling. I told Dee what was happening, and she said that she could tell something different was going on. Then the session began to get heavy, and was painful to me. I had to ask Michael to stop, and Dee pleaded with him too, but to no avail. He continued as if he did not hear us. Then, for some reason, Dee changed positions and the pain I was feeling was tremendously diminished. I don't know if she knew to do this intentionally or if Michael just gave her a nudge to do it, but immediately most of the hurt was gone.

This session went on for some time, and we both knew that

Michael had a reason for doing it. He told us that he had to finish what he had started. This occurs on occasion with the Angels so we understood what he meant. Not that it makes it any easier for us, but knowing that he is not just ignoring us helps with our understanding of the process. He did increase the intensity again, and I was in pain even with Dee taking most of it away, and we again asked him to stop. But, when we did this, he told me that this painful portion would not last too long. Dee said, "Does he mean he'll be finished soon?" I said, "No, he will just be finished with this painful part soon." And so he was. Shortly thereafter the pain subsided but he continued on with the session for a while longer. When he finally finished, we were both quite exhausted and fell into a very deep sleep for about another hour, which is par for the sessions that we are going through right now.

During the session Dee and I went to the Library and found a hallway. She was in front of me, pulling and hurrying me (as usual whenever we go there), and she opened all of the doors one by one. Apparently she was looking for a door that I had to enter to find another aspect of a past life that still needed attention. I told her that I felt I did not have to do that anymore, as I was finished with anything on the negative side that I needed to follow up on. However, she continued to open each door and told me to look in to see if I was drawn to it. Finally, we ran out of doors, and she was content. I clicked out after that point. It is good to know I have taken care of the negative aspects of my past lives so that I can move on without any excess baggage. That could prevent us from attaining some of the goals that we have set for ourselves in this life.

MICHAEL AND MY HEART

Dee:

As for the session with Archangel Michael pertaining to Rich's heart, let me first say that Rich had a doctor's appointment and he found that his heart rate was speeded up. I wanted to help in his healing so I asked for Michael's help and the Angels help in that matter. In the second where my body was used, I communicated with Archangel Michael that Rich's body could not withstand the vibration as yet, and said he could use my body. I told him to go through my body to get to Rich and be able to finish what needed to be done to Rich's heart. Before my body was used Rich was not able to handle the energy, and it was very painful for him. However, with me as a buffer of sorts, it was tolerable for him, and Michael was able to finish what was necessary.

(4/2/2006)

The past two days have been pretty bad for Dee and I. We have both endured tremendous pain in our bodies, mostly due to the weather. But, it could also be changes in our bodies. This morning we had a visit by a very powerful entity, neither of us knew who it was as Dee was not looking, and I could not tell. Dee said that she felt a lot of pressure coming to us, and I knew it was a powerful entity, but I could not put my finger on who it was. I do know that he was here for both of us because when he finished, I was told that we were now on a new track in our journey. What that means I don't know, but I had the idea that it would be different going forward. I had a feeling that it may have been Yeshuah who was here due to the high energy. It was definitely not Michael, as we know his energy signal. Dee could not say for sure, but my feeling could be right due to the message and the powerful experience that we were put through.

Dee:

There are so many times during the process of our sessions that I just go with the flow of what is happening. I have to, sometimes the energy coursing through my body and sending pain is too much to bear, and I don't have it in me to "tune in". I find myself not thinking about anything, just "being". This particular time was one of those, where I was not trying to see who was present, or feel who was present. It was like being a patient and accepting what was being offered. At the same time, I remember Rich asking me, "Who do you think it is?" Then saying, I hope this was for you. I don't like it when he does that. I said to him," I hope it was for the both of us." Knowing Spirit, I am sure it was.

(4/22/2006)

These days we have been experiencing many different energy flows from the Angel group. It seems that they have been taking turns, one at a time to do their own special part. Each one takes a turn then moves aside for the next one to come in and do another particular job. What exactly they are doing we do not specifically know, but we do know that they are working together for our good Of course, every once in a while, Raphael or Michael will show up and jump into the mix without any warning, but we are used to that. When Michael jumps into us it is usually for a specific reason. He will tell us that whatever he is doing has to be done. If we feel it is too intense or the session is too long, he will also tell us he has to finish what he started and give us an idea of how long that will take. But on occasion, when the session becomes too strong for me, we will ask him to either stop or come back another time. Sometimes Dee will offer that he can send the energy through her so that I am not overwhelmed by the increased energy.

Dee:

Rich has also been thrown back into a couple of past life experiences in the past sessions, and since the sessions have been flowing together lately it is hard to tell which one it was. I know that he will tell you the ones he does remember, but I remember that he was brought back to the Kahn lifetime once again, which means there is still something there that needs his attention. Of course, during that session the only word he said was "Kahn", and he was very disturbed, and wanted out. He then went through a few more lifetimes, but at the time, I had slipped deep and was gone as well. So, the next time I heard him I just assumed he was still in the same lifetime. Other than these glimpses, the sessions have basically been going on the same way, except for Archangel Michael's attire.

(3/26/2006)

Dee:

Rich and I woke up around 4 AM this morning, after having a couple of very tough days. My body felt as though if I didn't get back into bed quickly I would just drop, but at the same time, I was experiencing a great deal of pain. I couldn't function, so we headed back to bed. Almost immediately the angels showed up, and the first was a relatively new one, a being from the Pleiades named Enmenta. This being has been helpful of late with healing energies to my lower spine. When this being came in, something new happened. Through Rich a voice announced: I am George, I am a part of your higher self, and I am here to help you." Then he said, " Lay on Rich and we will go through the colors." He then proceeded to go through each chakra color, and I can only assume it was to clear and balance each one. I was in a very groggy state, when once again entities changed for Rich and I heard " I am Heimie, and I am here to protect you from the lower vibrating entities that surround you, do not worry, I will always protect you, you are a bright and shining light." These two types of experiences have never occurred to us before. Yes, we have had many angels and beings from different worlds, but we have never had any that claimed to be of our Higher Selves, nor of a protective nature.

62

Twenty Seconds

(5/11/2006)

Today while we were in the midst of two back-to-back sessions an entity that we have not seen for a while came charging back into our session with a vengeance. I call him Starman, but Dee has said his name is Gastin. He is from another galaxy, the Pleiades system. I do know when he is coming because his energy is so different. I can see this blue streak of light coming at me from somewhere out in the Cosmos, and I know he is going to be here in about three or four seconds. A lot of notice isn't it? I have time to grab hold of Dee and at least she knows that something dramatic is about to happen. Sometimes I can tell her to get ready, but other times there is no time, and she knows when I quickly change position and grab her, we are in for a something dramatic. When he comes, the energy is so strong I have to literally scream out. I try to place my head into a pillow so as not to scare the neighbors. The only good part about the whole thing is the session is very fast. I guess that is because the energy is so strong, he can get it over with quickly. However, sometimes, as in today's session there are two of them. Whenever the first is finished, I can tell if there will be a second one by the way my body feels. Then, I can tell Dee that they are not finished yet. Thankfully this type of session only lasts for about twenty seconds, but it is a very intense twenty seconds. I am also grateful that there are no residual effects from these. He comes, does his thing once or twice and then leaves so that we can get on with whatever else we have to do. We know when we will be affected by the different energies from the different entities and just how we will be affected.

(5/12/2006)

Last night Dee and I went through a different kind of session than we had been used to. We were both having episodes of extreme dizziness that even if we moved our heads a little bit we would be sent spinning out of control. This lasted for quite some time and neither of us could figure out why it was happening. Dee said that even if I spoke she would go spinning out again. This had never happened before to such a great extent.

After this subsided, I was sent falling into another time. This has occurred on other occasions, usually when I need to experience something from a past life. I was sent to this battlefield of death, which made me cry uncontrollably. I was not able to figure out a time frame, or what the multitude of dead and dying were wearing, or what battle implements they were using, but it was clear to me that this was a great battle where neither side seemed to have gained anything but the killing of many soldiers to no avail.

TWENTY SECONDS

(5/13/2006)

Last night the Angels seemed to be coming quite often throughout the night. Each time they came they would send a different Angel with a different energy signature but none of the Angels would stay very long. It was like they each took an inning in a ball game and then moved on. I was let go each time to come back to the present but then, a short time later, I would be taken again for another "inning" of their ball game. I felt badly doing this because naturally each time this occurred I would awaken Dee from her sleep and occasionally they were heavy sessions, and she would have to hold onto me and keep reminding me to control my breathing. She is quite used to this by now, but I just did not like the fact that I was disturbing her sleep because she does not get enough sleep as it is.

Even though the Angels come everyday to work with us, we are not always ready for what they throw at us, we really do love them for what they are doing. We would not change anything because we know it is for our own benefit. On the rare occasions that they may skip an evening, we actually feel lonely, or wonder if they will be back again, but they always come back. We are grateful for their help.

63

Costumes

(5/18/2006)

The other day during a session I saw Michael coming in wearing a costume, and I mentioned it to Dee. She said she knew. Afterwards, I asked her what Michael had been wearing, and I told her that I saw him wearing a full bandleaders outfit and carrying a baton for leading the band.

Dee:

This time Rich and I both saw Michael wearing different outfits! He saw him wearing a bandleader's outfit and I saw him wearing a Scottish plaid kilt (with the pin and all) and a ruffled, white long-sleeve shirt.

This episode reminded me of something I had read in one of Bruce Moen's books concerning his first meeting with Bob Monroe after Bob had passed on. Bruce said that Bob was as giddy as a kid in his new environment. I remember Bob saying to him that he had five or six different conversations going on at the same time, and he knew what was being discussed in each one at any given moment. This ties in exactly with what had just occurred to Dee and I with Michael. He can appear to me in one mode of dress while at the same time appearing to Dee in an entirely different mode of dress. I could see Dee seeing him in a Scottish outfit as she has some Scotch ancestry of which she is proud. Michael appears in different garb all the time. Sometimes he is flashy, and sometimes he is in normal dress, but when he's flashy Dee and I both know it right away. His energy is different when he is like that. I'd say it was brighter, and we both feel it when it happens. I'll mention it or she will. One of us just acknowledges it to the other.

Dee:

Michael was giving Rich an especially strong session, and I wanted him to stop. I asked Michael, "What is so important that you needed to do right at this moment?" He responded that there wasn't anything actually necessary. So, I asked, "You just wanted to get your licks in?" He asked me if I was angry, and I told him I was. The next thing I knew, all of the energies were thrown my way, and I was very dizzy. So I made a comment out loud saying "That's right, throw it all at me." I told him that we loved Him and all the Angels and appreciated all that they were doing for us, but right now he could wait until later in the evening. He got my message.

I sometimes get thoroughly exhausted during these sessions, but I do not like it when Dee takes on the energies that I am supposed to be dealing with. I feel that it is my job, and if I ask the Angels to take a break due to my physical exhaustion, I expect them to respect my request without them moving the energy to Dee. I will have to talk to Michael about this the next time I see him lurking around in the background.

64

Different Levels

I just finished another book on the afterlife that I thought was interesting. It went into what people do in Focus 27 after they pass from this Earth Plane. There was one part that I could really relate to, and I told Dee about it since it was something we had discussed recently. Dee and I have not been able to merge for many months now and merging is just about the most blissful thing that two people can experience. Dee had a conversation with Metatron the other day, and she asked him why we were no longer able to merge. He told her that we were above the vibrational level to do that anymore in the physical. She was pissed! She told him that was ridiculous since something so beautiful would no longer be able to be experienced by us. I thought it quite ridiculous also. I told her to take it up with some higher ups when she had the time, as she talks to the Angels on a daily basis. But, in reading this book on the afterlife, I found that there is more than one way to experience the merging process. In the book it stated that you normally merge using the heart chakra of the body, and there was another way to merge using the crown chakra of the body. However, it said that using the crown chakra is a much more involved process, and it leaves the people involved not knowing who they are for some period of time. It would seem possible this could only be experienced by two people who were totally out of the physical. We wanted to find out more about this because, if we are not permitted to merge through our hearts, we would be more than willing to merge through our crown chakras. Since we had experienced the heart chakra merging while still living in our third dimensional bodies that we currently reside in, it may be possible to experience this higher crown chakra level also.

Dee:

I had appealed to Metatron and asked him if we could merge once again like we used to as that experience is out of this world/ dimension. It is a total connection of unconditional love where both hearts are as one. You become "one heart", "one body", and "one soul" as you entwine and fly above and into the cosmos with and as one another. His answer surprised me, in that he said we were above that. He said that we have become one heart in the physical, but with no other explanation at the time. I was very upset. How in the world could we be above something so unbelievably divine in nature? I know that I will find out more information about this though, because this just doesn't seem right to me.

The other day we were discussing the above mentioned things in the car on the way home from Dee's mom's house. In particular Dee was explaining to me in detail what happened with Archangel Metatron and immediately at the conclusion of our discussion a song came on our IPOD from Van Morrison that was the ending song from the movie "Michael" which starred

DIFFERENT LEVELS

John Travolta as Archangel Michael. We both started laughing uncontrollably, and we knew that Michael had been listening to our conversation that had just concluded. You never know who is listening to you when you discuss anything, and you talk with Angels.

Dee:

When we were driving home, and had just finished our discussion on what had occurred with Archangel Metatron when the song "Bright Side of The Road" by Van Morrison from the movie "Michael" soundtrack came on. Now the thing is, we have our IPOD set up on shuffle, so it plays songs randomly. I am a firm believer in communication from many sources be it nature, radio, films, music, or TV. There are also messages from Angels, Guides, etc. You only need to be aware and be open to them.

(5/21/2006)

We had noted the variety of angels coming in to take their turns at every opportunity, which put some additional stress on my body. As each energy comes in different parts of my body are affected, and when the energies are the same or similar, my body can compensate. When the energies are constantly varying the degree, my body is affected tremendously. Be that as it may, I have been able to cope with it and continue to function. Dee does not like it at all, because she feels the Angels are taking advantage of me.

The newest area affected has been my abdominal area, and it is taking quite some time to get used to. You see, when they are working that area it feels somewhat like getting punched in the stomach, but it does not knock the wind out of me. I have become somewhat used to it, but I still feel some discomfort while experiencing this. I do not know what Angels are involved in this new area of adjustment as I have not been able to locate anyone new to the group; although I do get the distinct impression that someone is lying low just out of my line of sight Dee has not been able to pinpoint this new energy either.

Michael has been around too, as he frequently is, and I saw him on one occasion the other night just hanging out in the background watching what was transpiring. I knew he was up to something as he was just going around the group. He seemed to be waiting. When I saw him doing this I knew that he wanted to jump in. However, when the other Angels were finished he just sat back and did nothing. I do not know if he was just letting me have a respite from the session or why he was just sitting there waiting. After a few minutes of him doing nothing, I finally said, "Well, if you are going to jump in, let's get it over with." Before I was able to get that thought completed in my mind, he jumped in, which is not uncommon for him to do. As usual he takes charge of the situation and directs how things should go. This turned out to be a stronger session from him than I usually go through with his energy, and it continued for quite a while. When he was finished I was completely exhausted and had to sleep. Why Michael does some of these things I do not know. He is very cagey when it comes to answering questions about these sessions. Dee has much better luck finding out answers, as her connection is more direct when it

DIFFERENT LEVELS

comes to conversing with him. I speak to Michael myself on many occasions but it is more of me asking a question and getting an answer than an actual conversation as Dee has with him and the other Angels.

65

Sleepless Nights

(5/24/2006)

The other night the Angels were doing something that they had never done before, and I could not figure out the reason. They were pulling on my left arm, as they usually do when they want my attention to begin a session, but this time they were bothering me all night. Whenever I fell asleep, they would wake me up with a tug on my shoulder, even when I tried to hold Dee, so that they could start a session. However, they backed off and nothing would happen. This continued throughout the night getting me very frustrated. At one time I really hollered at them, but it did not make any difference. I could not figure it out, and I believe Dee had no answers for it either. In fact, they even continued the following night when I was at the firehouse. But, they were not bothering me throughout the night, only part of it. I still could not get much rest because when they would wake me I could not return to sleep for quite some time.

This past night both Dee and I were not feeling well due to the weather, and they left us alone until this morning when I was feeling somewhat better. I was nudged slightly, and I knew it was

Raphael bothering me. I told him to go away but, of course, he didn't listen. He jumped right in and put me through the paces for about fifteen minutes. Then he stopped, but he did not release me from his grip. I told Dee this, and she asked me if he was done. I said, "I think he is done, but he is still holding me." Prior to this, I had seen Michael pacing in the background waiting his turn. I saw Raphael sitting there holding me, and I did not know why. Dee said she asked him, and he said to her that he wanted to try something different on us. She also told him that Michael was waiting and that he might get mad if Raphael was just toying with us. We waited for a bit longer and all of a sudden Dee said she was very dizzy. I was feeling dizzy too but not to the same extent as Dee. Next, I felt the pain in my heart that is associated with Raphael. This was a similar pain to his normal session, but it continued up my left arm so it was different than a normal session with him. Dee's becoming dizzy was also not the normal state of affairs with his energy. This went on for a few more minutes and then he finally let us alone.

While resting after this session, I said, " Michael was just waiting to be asked to come in". Dee replied, "Yeah, and if we don't ask him, he'll just jump right in anyway." Dee said, "Did you see him smirk when I said that?" I had seen it and I told her so. Then I said, "As soon as I tell him it's ok to jump in, he will." As soon as I had that thought Michael jumped in. At least he sometimes has the courtesy to be asked before jumping in right after a previous session. I guess he is finally getting used to the idea that our physical bodies can only withstand so much energy from them before we get exhausted. That sure has been a long time coming! Now,

SLEEPLESS NIGHTS

if only the other Angels would learn that too. They still have no conception of time, especially when we tell them to come back later. To them that means two or three minutes, not an hour or so as we would desire.

66

Church Visit

(6/4/2006)

Today at church services at The Journey Within (where services are started with Spiritual Healing) something occurred to me that has only happened once or twice before. While I was sitting there meditating, I began to get very dizzy and I knew immediately that I was being taken to another location. So I thought to myself, let's see where we are going. Soon I was at a very tranquil and peaceful lake with a modest shoreline and trees all around. It was very serene and beautiful. As I looked around, who should be standing on the shoreline and smiling at me but Yeshuah. Immediately I understood why He was there, and why I was brought here on this occasion. I have been experiencing some turbulent times in my personal life at the moment, and He was there to let me know that He understood what was happening. He was always watching.

I was told that times like these were not always trials for me but may be for the others involved in these situations. Dee and I had discussed this between ourselves. Not all lessons that we encounter are for us, but may be for the other persons involved, and it was nice to know that we were on the right track. Being told by Yeshuah that we were just on the sidelines of a particular situation does not always make it easier since we are directly involved, but it is good to know that what we are doing is good and that we are not to blame for these occurrences happening at that particular time.

I find that with Dee by my side, we can handle anything that comes our way. The life experiences that either or both of us have experienced up to this point in our personal journeys have given us a unique perspective from which to observe the day to day travails of everyday life and for that we are most grateful.

67

One Soul

(7/27/2006)

A most interesting event just happened. Dee and I were having a session with the Angels and a totally new feeling began to descend on us. We both felt it and there was a new Angel involved too. Dee said the Angel was female. I could not get a sense, other than the Angel was someone we had not encountered before. As the session moved on, we felt we were entering new territory, an area that we had not been to before. I was able to communicate freely to Dee what was happening all through the session which is very unusual as I am many times prevented from speaking or communicating as I would like.

We were as one soul for the entire trip. Dee met up with this new Angel but did not get too much information. Our encounter brought us to an area of blissfulness that we had not been able to achieve since we were able to merge our spirits together. It seemed like eons ago. This connection was on a different plane of existence. We were in a new sphere, one that we had not encountered before. As we moved on during the session we found that we were closer than we had been able to get to in the past. Our souls were just one complete soul and our journey was completely connected! We seemed to be floating in time and space. I felt that we were moving from one dimension to another with the ease of a feather. We were being taken through different locations and times but were not affected in any way with these shifts.

68

Amah

(8/3/2006)

A new angel had appeared to us recently. She is the one who had a direct effect on both of us. When we start out in our sessions this Angel gets quite vocal and loud, through me, and Dee has told her to quiet down because she is so loud. I begin speaking in what Dee calls "Angel talk" because we cannot understand it. But this Angel speaks very loudly in full volume as if talking to someone. The interesting thing is that when she gets finished talking, Dee and I will be totally put into a very deep sleep for about an hour and a half. This occurs each time this Angel comes to visit with us. The first few times this happened we really did not understand that it was even happening, but when it continued, we could see something very different was happening to us. During the first few times this Angel showed up, I would keep saying the word "Amah." I did not know why, but when I told Dee to ask this new Angel what her name was, she said that indeed her name was Amah meaning Mother Earth. She is an Indian woman with a long braid of black hair, dark skin and eyes. Now, we had a new friend in the spiritual world but still did not know what her purpose was.

(8/ 9/2006)

This morning, while we were deep within another session with the Angels, we experienced yet another and different sensation. During the first portion of the session I was extracting pain from Dee. When that ended and we changed positions, I felt that Dee was taking energy into herself from my body. At first energy was moving from my legs into her and after a while this sensation moved up from my legs to my torso. It went on for quite some time, and I mentioned to her that the session was different from others. She agreed. Finally, the sensation became a whole body feeling, not unlike others that we have experienced before. I was being drained of energy during this entire time, and I knew that sleep would follow directly afterwards. When the Angels had finished this session and left us I was completely wiped out. I ended up sleeping for another two hours to let my body recuperate and get back to normal.

69

Dee's Illness

(9/1/2006)

Today I decided to go on a journey to Focus 23 through Focus 27 to see what has been going on. I had not done this for quite sometime, and I was not sure that I would be able to access the area again. I always have trepidation about doing something like this after a prolonged respite. I feel a bit like Bruce Moen when he had to convince himself that it was for real when he could not comprehend it.

When I started out in Focus 21, everyone as usual was at the Cafe. Thomas and his big bright smile was sitting at a table with that look of his that he already knows what is going to happen. Thomas lives on a higher plane. I decided to take a trip with Dee to see where we could go. As we crossed over the Bridge to Focus 23 I asked my guide to direct me to anyone who might need assistance today. I was not feeling directed to anywhere special so we moved on to Focus 24 and through to Focus 27 with no tugging at us to stop along the way. I was somewhat surprised that we were not pulled onto a level to assist anyone, but I figured that Spirit knew what it was doing.

TALKING WITH ANGELS

Upon entering the Park, Dee and I made our usual stop at the willow tree, which was again an extraordinary experience especially since the Angels have not allowed us to merge for ages. They have said that we have risen above that now, but they still do not understand what being in the physical is all about. We simply cannot explain it to someone who has never experienced it. Anyway, we approached the Center, and I asked Dee where she wanted to go. She had no place in particular so I said, "Let's go to the Library and see what happens."

When we arrived at the Library, I wanted to look into a past life of Dee's to see why she is experiencing the pain in this lifetime. She told me that would be fine with her. We wandered over to the Past Life section of the Library, and we came across a scroll dated 624 AD. I said, "This must be it", and we proceeded to that time period. The first impression that I received was one of an extremely barren time. The area felt like Europe, but during this time there were no cities or buildings. Everyone just seemed to be barely scratching out an existence. I saw Dee in what amounted to rags around her body with nothing on her feet. It felt cold to me, and I could not understand how she could stand it with no shoes on. Of course, if there were even shoes available at this time, they were probably only for those who could afford them, and it seemed most of the people around were not able to afford anything. It was a totally hardscrabble existence. After watching the scene, I saw Dee come into contact with a person that I could not fully see but their appearance was one of darkness. As she approached this person she was asked if she would like to have all the food and clothing that she needed. She was in very desperate straights and wanted to know what the cost would be. She was told that there would be a cost but that she could afford it. Not believing this she continued on for a while but eventually she came back to look for this person. Finding him and in a state of starvation she said that whatever the cost would be she was willing to pay it since she had nothing but the rags that she was wearing.

At this point I asked for guidance as to what the cost was and how she was going to pay it. Getting no answer I called upon my Angel guides and the one who showed up was Madagascar. I thanked her for coming and asked, "Why can't I get any more information about this meeting and timeframe of Dee's life?" She simply said, "Dee hasn't given me permission to see what happened". I was truly blown away by that statement because it was so totally unexpected at the time. I sat there dumbfounded and said there must be a reason, but for the life of me I could not understand it. So I was left with knowing this was the timeframe of why Dee is experiencing what she is going through now, but I had no explanation for it. All I could do was to speculate as to what the deal may have been.

(9/8/2006)

A thought popped into my mind about who the person was and what the transaction was between Dee and him. It was like a lightening bolt hitting me. I was the person! I was taken aback by this prospect, but I thought about everyone's past lives and that we all had experienced times that we wish had not happened.

This appeared to be part of one of my past lifetimes. It started to make sense to me especially when thinking about the fact that Dee had not given me permission to see this, and I could not perceive the person but only a shadow of him. I feel she was trying to protect me from knowing this at the time. I still do not know exactly what the deal was, but from what I now know, I can see why it is so important for me to help Dee get well. It would seem that I had something to do with the reason she is ill in this lifetime.

(9/11/2006)

Upon further reflection on the above matter, it appeared that a deal was struck with Dee so that she would be able to live a fruitful existence in that lifetime but that a payment would be due down the road in a future lifetime. This lifetime appears to be that future for her, and for me. As I said, I felt I had done an injustice to Dee at that time and that I would pay for it in the future as well. It seemed to me that future was now. This must also be the reason we are so close to each other in this lifetime. We are both paying for our past indiscressions. Neither of us is exactly sure of what the deal was, and how the future will play out, but we will handle anything that comes our way together and that makes all the difference.

70

Healing Hearts

(10/15/2006)

The session with the Angels this morning was a continuation from yesterday. Yesterday, we were at a class with Tom Cratsley from Lily Dale, NY. He gives Spiritual classes and came down to New Jersey for a Healing Heart Class that was offered by our church. I did not think of it before the class, but I should have known. A class like opening up the heart to better understand our surroundings and ourselves would be a perfect opportunity for the Angels to jump in. Sure enough, they were there chomping on the bit. Early in the day we were doing a meditation to open our hearts to our surroundings. With that opening for the Angels, they were right there trying to get into the picture. I was sitting next to Dee on a sofa and holding her hand, and it gave them an even easier venue. There was another person sitting on the sofa with us, and I tried not to make it too obvious what was going on. Dee immediately picked up on this and tried to tell the Angels that this was not the right time for them to be coming in. Of course, they do not like to be told to come back later, so they continued with their antics. I was trying my best to keep them at bay or get them to go away, but they were very persistent. My body was shaking much more than I would have liked, and they continued to the end of the meditation exercise.

When the meditation was over Dee asked, "What did they want?" I told her Michael was trying desperately to come in, but I did not know why. I asked her to find out why he needed to come in now. She excused herself from the class for a few minutes, and when she came back, she told me that he wanted to finish what he had started the other day and did not complete at that time due the fact that my physical body could not tolerate anymore during that particular session. Dee said she told him that we were in a class and that he could not come in in front of all these people. She tried to explain to him that if he did, it would not be the right time. She hoped that he understood. She told him that he should cool it until we had gotten home for the evening. However, at the time we were not sure he would do so. Fortunately, we went on to other areas of opening up the heart and finding source, so without even thinking about him anymore, we were able to push through it without being interrupted by him again. Michael did not even come into my mind for the rest of the day until we were traveling home and I told Dee it was nice of Michael not to have bothered us.

The class itself was very good. I learned more about myself and how to tune into others, which was not the real idea of the class, but that is what it turned out to be for me. During one of the first group events we were told to match up with a partner and sit across from that person. We did this several times throughout the day always changing partners. When I matched up with Tom

Cratsley the exercise was one of first going deep into our own heart and then moving across to our partner's heart and trying to feel their energy within their heart. Then, we were to expand our perception to the area around this person, to their aura more or less, and gather whatever impressions we could.

When we were finished and it was time to discuss our interpretations, Tom immediately said to me that my heart was so full of love, and that I was sharing it with the world around me and with everyone I met. I was surprised because that was totally unexpected especially from someone I did not even know. Tom went on to say that I was the calm within the storm during trying situations and could keep things on an even keel. I understood what he meant and at that point I told him that I was a firefighter and that calmness in the middle of a storm is commonplace for all firefighters. He said, "Yes, that might be, but you have a special knack for keeping things smooth in difficult situations." I thanked him for his kind words.

Next, it was my turn to give Tom my impressions of him. I had not ever done anything like this before so I just had to go with what my impressions were. I do know enough about this area of the dimensional-spiritual world to know that we must not try to analyze or second-guess ourselves because analyzing is just the left-brain coming in and distorting things that come from right brain activity. The first thing I felt from him was the idea that what he was doing was very special. His work in this area meant a lot to many many people. He was in the right place, doing the right thing. Of course, he already knew this but that is what I was feeling. When we were directed to open our awareness to the area around the person I saw an elderly woman standing over his right shoulder. She said that she was always there with him, and that she was very proud of him. I told him this, and he said she was his grandmother and she shows up many times for him in these types of situations. He knows she is always there by his side with great love and admiration for what he is doing.

I was somewhat taken aback by this because this was not what we were supposed to be looking for during this exercise but this is what I perceived. I said to Tom that I am not psychic and not a medium and this was my first venture into this area. I told Dee about this episode later on, and she said that maybe I am a medium after all. She said we all have the ability to do mediumship -- it is just a matter of opening up ourselves to the possibilities. However, mediumship is nice but it is not one of my passions to pursue. My avenues of going through the veil are similar to mediumship only slightly different. I suppose they're just different focus levels.

We did the same exercise with a different partner and this time I perceived from this person's heart little children around her and a playground area. There was tremendous love coming from her to these children. She later told me that she does work with children, so once more I was going in the right direction. I also saw an older gentleman over her shoulder, and she told me that was her grandfather, and he is often around her.

What I have found during these exercises was that when we open our perception to others around us, we perceive many aspects of our own lives too. This is an area that may hold some interest for me down the road, but for the time being, I am still working with the Angels to make Dee well and that consumes much of my time. We work on healing constantly, and we know that one day she will be well. Until then we let the Angels do what they need to do to further us along that path.

71

Cozumel

(11/11/2006)

When we returned from our trip, the Angels began a new series of sessions with us. This new series is entirely different from any we have experienced in the past, and we have not had a session change in quite some time.

The first thing that happened was while Dee was lying on top of me the Angels showed me a picture of a heart. This heart was in very fine detail and was a heart very sick with disease. I could see that a majority of this heart was dead. It looked like a tree that had died with the branches withered and twisted about. I knew that this represented Dee's heart and also represented her whole body, not just her heart per se. I could perceive that the damage to this heart represented all of the problems that were going on inside of Dee. It might have frightened someone who did not understand what the representation was, but I intuitively knew that this was a representation of her ill body in the state that it was now in.

Thinking about it now, I really should have been upset due to the fact that we have been working together for almost two years now on healing with the Angels and this showed me that we had not made much progress. Dee has always said that the time must not be right for her to be healed when I would mention this fact. She is always optimistic as I am most of the time, but sometimes we all get disappointed when we do not see results with something that we have been working so hard to achieve.

There was something about this picture that made the whole process worthwhile and that was the fact that behind this heart I could see a bright golden light. This I knew was the light of love from God. He was showing me that Dee had not been forgotten and that we were on the right track with what we have been doing. Indeed, there was a light at the end of this long and dark tunnel. I was immediately filled with an overwhelming feeling of love due to this light and I knew that something was about to change.

As I was taking all of this in, I realized that Dee had fallen asleep. I can always tell when she falls asleep because her body begins to twitch in little subtle ways. I went on to just relax and go with the flow of what was happening, but after a while I felt that I did not feel any energy flowing either into or out of Dee or me. This is unusual as I always can tell when there is energy present from the Angels. I thought at first that maybe they were finished for this session and that was the reason I felt nothing. Then, the information came into my mind that this is the way these types of sessions would be going forward. Dee would be asleep, and I would be awake but not really feel anything going on between us. I was told that there was great healing for Dee at this point, but that I would be the quiet conduit during these healings. I did not question this as I have learned that when information pops into my head it is correct information and there is a reason for things even when I do not understand.

When this session was over, I was again shown this picture of a very sick heart with the golden light behind it, but I noticed that at the very tip of one of the thin wretched looking branches that there was a very subtle sign of life. It looked as if a little touch of green and yellow had come into this very tiny branch, and I knew right then this was going to be the start of Dee's true healing process. From the very slight indication of life being breathed back into this heart I knew it was going to be a very long process, but the process had finally begun. I am praying that this type of indication will continue to be shown to me so that I can monitor it.

(11/13/2006)

Over the course of the next few days I was shown how this new process is going to work. When the Angels want to start one of these particular sessions I get a feeling within my body that is different from the usual feeling that I have experienced. It is so distinctive that I know what they want us to do. Even if we are just sitting on the couch together, I get a very strong feeling within my heart of being tugged, pulled, and/or drawn into a new session. I told this to Dee and she said "now?" and I said, "You know the Angels" meaning that they have no concept of time or conditions in our reality. They just want what they want when they want it. This time, since were just at home it really didn't matter, but on occasions they become a pest when they interfere with other things that we may be doing.

When we set ourselves up for this session I found that Dee was not really ready to sleep. I indicated this to the Angels and told them that the only way that they were going to get Dee to fall asleep right now was to have Amah come in and put her to sleep. Usually Amah will put both of us to sleep, but somehow I knew that Dee would sleep and I would not. This was due to the fact that I was told previously that Dee would sleep through these sessions, and I would be awake. Amah came in immediately and shortly thereafter Dee was off to dreamland. I was conscious the whole time and again I could not feel any changes within my body. These sessions last longer than most, even up to an hour in length, but I do not mind since these are healing sessions for Dee. She is what is most important and my comfort or concerns come a very distant second.

Dee later on said, "Why can't you sleep during these sessions as the Angels in the past have done work while we both were asleep?" I told her this is different from the past sessions and they had told me that I was going to be awake during these types of sessions, and she should not worry about me.

When the session was over, I was again shown the picture of the heart with the golden light behind it, and I could see that there was a slight increase in the greenish yellow portion of one of the branches indicating that there was life flowing back into this heart and we were going forward. This is what makes the whole thing worthwhile. I am so grateful that they are showing me progress for what we are doing. The whole idea of this has always been to help Dee get well and with that goal constantly in sight we will continue to do whatever is needed to reach it. The love that we have for each other just continues to grow and helps us to deal with each day. We constantly thank God and all the Angels for their help along this path.

(11/15/2006)

I have to put this in at this point even though Dee has not yet met the new Angel. The other morning during the session described above I asked who the new Angel was. Who would be working with us at this point? I immediately was told he was a Spirit Guide and his name was Mantasooran. That name was quite different from what I expected since Amah's name was quite easy to remember. Since this is what I was told, I said fine. I went to look for him, and I was shown what Mantasooran looked like. He was of average height with a long flowing gray beard and long gray hair, wore a robe and walked with a cane that had a handle like a "T" on it. He was genuinely jolly and said he would help us along on this part of our journey. He did not feel like a sorcerer type, and he acknowledged that he was not one. I asked him why he used a cane since he was in the Spiritual Realm and did not need it. He advised me that when he was in the physical he used a cane similar to the one he had and that he liked it and wished to use one here in this realm. I thought that was interesting and let it go at that.

72

The Field

(11/29/2006)

While I was in bed an entity decided to come barging into my awareness. I recognized the energy as a Starman type of energy, in other words from the Pleiades star system. I was able to say to Dee "Starman" so she would be aware of who was there, because the Starman energy is extremely intense. It makes Michael's energy look tame in comparison. When the entity started I did not feel the normal intensity that Starman usually comes with. I began to feel a separation of my body and spirit. I told this to Dee and she said, "Well, that's not good." I told her it would be okay as he was the one doing it and not for any "bad" purpose.

When the separation began I could still feel both sides of my being, the physical and the spiritual although I could still feel the difference between the two. This had happened previously to me so I was aware of the feelings involved, but I did not know why he was doing this. About this time it also occurred to me that the entity was not Gastin whom usually comes from the Pleiades, but another entity. I could not remember Gastin's name at the time so I just told Dee that it was not Starman and she understood. I kept getting a name, Negron, during the whole process so I guess the entity's name was Negron. I found out afterwards that it was.

While experiencing this separation process I was not aware of its purpose and I was told that he would explain it to Dee. With the reason covered for the session I just went with the flow and was able to tell Dee that they would explain it to her. I kept getting the following timeframe in my mind, but I am not entirely sure which time they were referring to: it was either 2,000 to 2,300 or it was 22,000 to 23,000 years ago. I am not certain. My spirit was being turned around and shifted in many directions. I did not understand why, and when I asked, I was told that Dee would understand.

My sprit was transported out into the universal cosmos. That is a most exciting place because you can sense and feel the experience. Just understand the "feeling" is one of exquisite oneness with all that there is. Recently I have done some reading indicating that this area is called "The Field" and that scientists are beginning to understand that everything in "The Field" is a oneness to everything and everyone else in the cosmos. In other words, we are all one with everything and everyone in the entire universe. This is a new concept for many scientists, and they are having great difficulties coming to terms with it. Many of us that are spiritual do understand this is really the way it is. Many new experiments with the mind have generated much data proving that this is the way consciousness works. Of course, some scientists still doubt it.

73

Dad Again

(12/9/2006)

As I write this I am trying to recall all of the events that happened during this encounter. It started out as if I was falling. Now, when this happens it usually means the Angels are taking me to a place where something different is going to occur. What it is or where it will occur I never know until I get there. As I was traveling it appeared that I was going through space and at first I thought that I was being taken to another planet or another dimension.

Anyway, as I was slowly coming to a stop I viewed a vast beach with beautiful pinkish-sand and palm trees blowing in the breeze. The sky was a rich blue color, quite different than what we usually see here on Earth. However, the most interesting part of the whole scene was that I could not see an ocean. There may have been one, but it was cut off from my view, which was strange because I realized I was standing directly on the beach. The area where the ocean should have been was just a very dark black area. It was not frightening or intimidating, but it was strange.

As I was gaining my perspective I saw my father walking towards me on the beach. I had not seen him or spoken to him for some time, and I did want to speak to him, so I guess the Angels figured this was the right time to bring us together. He was wearing kaki pants with one of those tropical shirts from the 1950's that he always loved. It was also a beige type of color, and he was wearing sandals. His outfit totally took me by surprise, but I was very pleased to see him again. I walked over to him and gave him a huge hug that lifted him off his feet. He looked perfectly well and happy in this environment, especially since he was always an avid seafarer when he was alive, so this meeting place fit him to the tee.

He said that he knew that I had wanted to talk to him for a while and now was the proper time to meet. He seemed to know all of the questions that I was looking to find answers to, and he took them one by one, pretty much even before I asked them. He said that the current things that are giving me grief in my life right now will pass; therefore, do not dwell on them.

Dad told me that Dee and I have many great things ahead of us but not quite yet. One of the most important things he said was that Dee will be well in the future. This is always on my mind, and I am continually trying to make her as comfortable as possible and doing healing as much as I can for her. There has been a change recently in Dee's pain area moving from one place to another, but that is not a cure, it is a change. Dee said the Angels told her that she did not perceive these changes properly. She was told that her back is not bothering her as it was before, but she contends that now her hip is in a lot of pain. They said to her that she should be grateful that her back does not hurt. They said that these are part of the process that she has to go through to be completely healed. Of course, no time frame was given nor was any detail as to what to expect next in the process. But at least they told her that this was a positive change in her condition and not a negative one.

Another thing mentioned by my Dad was the fact that Dee and I are where we should be right now. We have heard this before, and we have to just accept this as the way it is. We will have to wait a little longer for the great things ahead for us.

74

New Teachings

As we moved into 2007, we noticed that there was a change in the energies coming in during our sessions. The Angels started to come in less and less, and in their place were these entities who introduced themselves as "Light Beings". Dee asked them how they were different from the Angels, if they were at a higher station or vibratory rate than the Angels, and she was told no, they were "just different". They told us that we were moving forward, or onto other things now, and that there were many who wanted to come to us. I do have to say that our Angels were always present during these times, almost as if watching over us. We came to find that for the most part, the Beings of Light all had names of only 2 letters, such as Po, Ra, Do, So, No, Pi, and there were many more. Also we were introduced to more "Star Beings" at this time who were also here to help us in our journey to move forward, and they also told us there were many of them who wanted to come to us as well. It was easier for the Star Beings to communicate than the Light Beings for some reason or other, and they told us that the reason everyone was so interested in us, was because to them we were "special", and that there are not many like us here, that are of "one heart", "one soul". We could always tell the difference between the Star Beings and the Light Beings, it wasn't just the difference in their energies, but the Star Beings would always come in calling "Anya". As Anya, you know, is Dee's original name, and we would come to find that a lot of the Star Beings had known her, either in previous life times, or from her home planet.

This year was a very busy time for us, but for the most part our spirituality took the number one spot in our lives. That is between looking for a new home in Arizona while still living in New Jersey, taking care of Dee's Mom who lives 2 hours away from us, working as a full time firefighter, and helping out at our church store "The Angel Within". On our next trip to Arizona we decided to go to the eastern/central area, a place called "The White Mountains", where Dee had heard there were some very nice spiritual energy, and this time we were ready to look at homes that were for sale. We had searched the surrounding area of Sedona, up to Flagstaff on our last trip, and nothing really had called to us there. We were on Rte. #60 driving in from Show Low, and as we came over the mountain the sight took our breath away. We are not sure if it is the reason why they are called the White Mountains or not, but everywhere your eyes could see everything looked "white". It was because of the reflection of the sun on the grass, which was almost the color of winter wheat, but I am talking rolling mountains here, as far as your eyes can see, interrupted here and there by some sage brush, rocks, and mountain tops, so very beautiful. We knew we had found our new home. As we were coming into the little town, dizziness hit us with all the spiritual energy of the place. Spirit worked miracles as usual, in us finding a home that was just perfect for us and Dee's Mom that wasn't on our list, and we put down a contract on it and returned home. Retirement as a firefighter would have to come first before us moving to our dream home in Arizona.

Both the Light Beings and the Star Beings told us that the place we were moving to was sacred land, holy land, that the land there was ancient, and also said something about our ancestors living there. We were told that we would be met not only by other Light and Star Beings once we moved, but that our ancestors would also be there to greet us, and help us to move forward in our journey. They also said that we have much work yet to do, and that the people will come to us.

In Sept.2007, we planned a trip to England to visit Dee's best friend Karen, (Kasha, the Angels call her), and about a month before we went we were introduced to a Light Being named Jo. This Light Being just happened to love our Shaman's Heart hemi-sync CD, and he was a particular teacher of ours, as he was teaching us how to show others what they termed "The One". It is what Dee and I have attained already here in the physical, and the Beings say that at some point in time, it is how all of humanity or all on Earth will be. Our particular task at this time is to give "The One" to Karen while we are in England, and Jo is coming to help us learn how to give this to others. He also informed us that once Karen has "The One", she can use her own discernment in giving those she feels are ready to receive it as well. Jo explained that not all will be ready even though we may feel they are; it is then they will need to work with Yeshua in order to bring themselves to where they need to be. The best way to explain this giving of "The One" is I go into a trance like state and Dee connects her heart to mine. Then depending on how well you know the person, they can either connect to Dee's heart, (heart to heart) or they can put their hand on Dee's heart. After Karen, we have only been asked to give "The One" to one other person, and that was Dee's son Chris. Dee had never been to Europe so it was wonderful for her to experience, and we stayed with Karen and Michael, who took us to Stonehenge, Avebury, and this wonderful little town where all the horses run (walk) free.

(Oct.2007)

No sooner had we gotten back from England, than the Beings were starting to tell us that they wanted us to leave New Jersey, and move to our new place. I hadn't planned on retiring until March of 2008, but they were being insistent on this issue, without really giving us any kind of other information. So now I had to figure out what I could do as far as my retirement goes, as well as work out moving 2 locations, and Dee had to plan a quick wedding. We had planned on getting married at our own church where we had met before moving to Arizona. Where there is a will there is a way! The Beings of Light had given us up to the first week of December 2007, but they preferred we leave the last week of November 2007. During all the sessions with the Light and Star Beings they made mention of the fact that they liked the "noise" (music), which we always had playing. Sometimes, more often than not, they would interfere with the Bose CD player/

alarm clock, and during the session, it would either, shut itself off and turn on again, or the volume would go up and down. Most of these sessions dealt with giving "The One" to the Beings themselves, and the reaction of most of Light Beings was one of never having felt anything like it before, as they explained they had never been in physical form. However, the reaction of the Star Beings was totally different, most would say, they haven't felt anything like this in such a very long time. Or they would say much, much, long ago. The speech coming through was very rough English, just words put together haphazardly, the best way they could. At first it was very hard for them to even breathe through my body, and Dee would have to calm them down, and help to bring their vibration down enough to fit into my physicality. She would have to explain the "in and out" of the lungs to the "Beings of Light" so that they could breathe for me while they were in my body, and they would argue with her, they didn't want to do it. They said it wasn't necessary (not in those words of course), she would have to explain to them that in order for me to survive they would have to do it, because I was still in the physical. That it may not be necessary for them, but for me it was. Dee would get so used to having to explain that when a Star Being came in, and she would start to say, "in and out" they would just say, "I know", me do it" because Star Beings have been in physical form and do know how to breathe.

(Nov. 2007)

This is the month that everything is happening in our lives.

TALKING WITH ANGELS

I am retiring from 25 years of service with the fire department, Dee and I are getting married, and we are moving to Arizona. If that isn't pressure I don't know what is. Well, the retiring part is easy it's all the rest that has to get done in a relative short period of time. In the midst of all of this we have been taking Dee for procedures in NYC. They are called radio frequencies, and her doctor does them under a fluoroscopy machine. She has had three done in the past couple of months due to severe pain in her hips and legs, which not only have been keeping her awake at night, but is also impairing her ability to walk. Dee is not discouraged by any of this at all she feels that before you get better you go through trials of tougher times. She is now feeling better than she was, and back to her "normal" stable. I have gotten all of the moving plans situated and ready, and Dee has gotten all of the wedding plans organized. We picked up our marriage license, got all of our decorations, everything is packed and ready for Arizona so we are ready to go. All we have to do now is get married, go to DMV, and the municipal building to tie up the loose ends, and we will be off on our journey. I'd like to thank my Uncle Carmine for accepting to be my best man, and Dee's son Chris for accepting to stand up for her at our wedding, we couldn't have asked anyone more precious to us than the both of you. The wedding was wonderful, and now we are also legal on paper, as one! Dee wanted a renaissance type of wedding, so we had one, nothing real fancy though. We only have a few days before having to head off to Arizona, which means only a few days to get everything we need done accomplished. I have faith that we will do it, all in good time.

NEW TEACHINGS

The moving trucks have arrived. Yesterday we were in Southern Jersey helping the movers load up Dee's Mothers belongings. Today, it is our turn, and it will be our final day in New Jersey. After the truck is loaded, we will pick up Dee's Mom, and head out west and onto the next chapter in our lives. I would really be remiss if I didn't mention a certain Star Being named Ponch, and, two Light Being's, Na and Wa. Ponch has been so very helpful, and seems to be a Star Being who has been assigned to watch over our children. I know I have mentioned before that he calls Dee's son "Small One". If you know Dee's son, it is laughable, because he is 6'3" tall, is very stocky, built young man, but Ponch has been watching over him, and has been protecting him, even if it is from his own self. Ponch would come through with a warning, if he shouldn't drive that night, or the next night, or if he shouldn't go out after work, things of that nature. Ponch would also come through and let Dee know if something was wrong with her son, or if he was going down the wrong path, and needed someone to give him a little kick, or a hug. He has also come through with some news of the other children, my children, also Karen's children and grandchildren. The only problem we have with Ponch is that he just LOVES "The One", he gets so excited when he comes in, that he jumps all around, and wears me out he expends so much energy. Wa is a Being of Light that actually came from one of the standing stones at Avebury (the Barber stone) in England. Dee took a picture of the Barber stone and you can see the energy in the picture. When we got home, Wa came through, and told us where he came from, he has been with us ever since, and has helped us, has warned us and given us warnings for those in the family as well as for Karen (Kasha) and her family. The same goes for Na, only he has been around much more than Wa. They both have come through with many different things to say, or advice to give.

Throughout the years there have been many different Angels, Arch Angels, Light Beings, Star Beings, and Entities from different planets, different planes or dimensions and realities. We have discovered so many of our past lives shared, and not shared. There is so much to be discovered within your own consciousness, your own being ness, the Universe exists within "YOU". Each and every one of you has the power of perception, and of opening up your mind to every possibility. Dee and I both know that all these things are true and happened to us, are still happening to us, and are open and available to others as well. If there was one thing I felt needed to be said, needs to be heard, is that we are all "ONE". You've heard that before, I know, but have you heard there is more to it? It is a connection, a connection of heart and soul, and all of us, not only all of us, but everything will have that connection back again someday like it was before. That is what "They" say. "Like it was before", and hasn't been in a very long time. It will start with merging like we did. We hope you find something you can gain from our story, and if not then we hope you at least had some fun.

It continues....

NOTE:

The following Epilogue was added by Dee beginning on August 2, 2008:

EPILOGUE

Dee:

Our journey began in this lifetime long before our meeting in the physical. It seems that Divine providence had plans for us, and we must also have had these plans for ourselves.

We have come to find out that we spent many other lifetimes together and, then again, many that we did not share. I had been going to, and was a part of a Spiritualist Church for many years, and had been told by some people that the person I would some day meet was already in my energy field. At that time, I had thought it would be more like a guy I would normally pick. However, I had been told it would be someone I would meet at my church. A few years went by, and within that time I had a few dreams and visions where I was shown who I was going to be with. The only catch was I was never shown his face!

I was told by my Angels he would be a man I would not normally be interested in; he would be different than all the rest; and I was not to choose on the basis of what had been normal for me. In January of 2005 things started to change. By that time I questioned the Angels as to when this mystery man would appear in my life.

It started after Rich, who attended my church, went to a gateway program at The Monroe Institute and began to go on journeys in the Astral. He decided to share some of his experiences with some members of the church by email. I enjoyed reading his journeys, and I liked the way he wrote about them. I found that I couldn't wait for him to take his next journey or to see him on Sunday. Before his emails I had seen him at church a few times and knew of him, but I thought he was married. Like the Angels said, Rich was a clean cut, straight laced, more of a yuppie type guy and I would normally go for a tattooed, rough and tough kind of guy. As it turned out, I started to turn up in Rich's journeys. He would be doing a soul retrieval and all of a sudden I would be there. It seemed that if he got into a tough spot or needed assistance with someone he was trying to help, I would show up to help him.

We started to travel together in the Astral Realm, and there was a distinct soul connection between us, so much so that there were things happening in the Astral that we weren't remembering when we returned to the Earth Plane. One day, I had feelings of being intimate with Rich when I returned to the Physical Realm, and I wanted to know if he was doing this to me on purpose, or if he was also unaware. I put it to him as delicately as possible. He was shocked, and didn't know what I was talking about. I was relieved.

However, it came to pass that we were very active in the Astral Realm together as our souls are one and couldn't get enough of one another.

After that we decided to get together in the Physical and see how it went. Since then it has been a fairytale. What the Angels had shown me in my dreams and visions happened the first weekend we were together. Words were spoken, and scenes were played out. We were destined to be with one another (or should I say back together

EPILOGUE

again?). Not only could we not be out of each other's sight or energy fields for too long, but the Angels and our Spirit Guides had plans for us. The plans were mostly for Rich at the beginning because they told us that he had to be brought up to my level of vibration.

The shifts began with the help of our Angel group and Archangel Michael. We had so many interesting experiences and we came to find out we were together since the beginning of creation. We have spent many past lives together and have experienced within our present lifetimes the most glorious spiritual reunion – people today term it "Twin Flames". Through the merging of our energies, and our hearts, and souls it has become a new way of experiencing.

Before Rich and I were together, I would get messages or daily communications from my Angels, and also in dreams and visions. Right before we got together in the physical sense, I was told that my teaching or learning would be halted. I thought this was a bit unfair at the time. However, they were letting me know that were Rich and I to get together, certain things had to be done first in order for us to proceed together in a spiritual sense. At the time they stopped they were about to show me how to move through the dimensions while still in my physical body. I had many dreams of ascending (floating upwards) and coming back down, being partially invisible and partially solid, after being in a horrible accident, explosion, gun shot, and then being absolutely all right, etc. I also had many futuristic dreams as well, where I was shown places as they would look in the future, which did come to pass, and dreams of which I am hoping do not come to pass that all have to do with the major Earth changes taking place.

But that was before I knew Rich, and I had a lot of work to do.

I honestly had no idea what was in store for us. I have never felt the kind of unconditional love for anyone (other than my son) that I felt for Rich and still do. With Rich, of course, it is a total love and our Creator/God certainly knows what he/she is doing. Believe me, if anyone has ever experienced what we have experienced, there is no denying the existence of our beloved Creator, and the unconditional love that permeates the universe.

During our sessions I noticed that the Angels would call me Anya. This happened not just once but all the time. As the sessions progressed, I finally asked at one point why I was being called Anya. I was told that Anya was my "first name" or "angel name". Since that time I have been told that Rich's first name was "Abrahama" and my friend Karen's first name is "Kasha. Her husband Michael's first name is "Mordone." These are the only formal names they use. When the Angels refer to my son Chris, they call him "small one", and if they are trying to relate something about one of Karen's grandchildren, they will tell me "tiny red one" for her grandson who has red hair, just to give you an idea of how messages will come through to me if they are meant for certain people.

Each and every session has a purpose and either a learning experience or a message involved. There was a time when the Angels kept shifting Rich's vibrations. This was after Archangel Metatron had come in. Every time I asked them to please give him a break, I was told that it had to be done now. The Archangel Michael was primarily doing the work and a lot of adjusting was being done to his DNA/RNA as well as to his vibratory rate. It got to the point where Rich's whole body went stiff and, all of a sudden, I could barely hear him breathing. I became a bit nervous, and I started to softly *call Rich's name. There was no response! I wasn't prepared to see him like that, and I started to freak out.*

I began begging Archangel Michael to do something. I was told it had to be that way, and it was a necessary step. Suddenly, Rich came out of it with a huge intake of breath! The first thing Rich said to me was that he had seen a pair of feet in dusty sandals standing on his chest. He felt for some reason Yeshuah was preparing him to either breathe under water, or see how long he could keep his body temperature low, and breathing just as low.

Throughout our times in the sessions a few of the Entities that have come in have said to me, "You talk to Big One." At first I was a bit unsure of what they were trying to say. Most of the time they would say," You talk Big One", and I had to figure out what they were trying to tell me. Afterwards I figured out, they mean I talk to the Creator/God. I would then say, "Yes you're right" to them. When I tried to get into conversations with them to see what questions I could get answered, most of their answers were very cryptic. The questions they did answer, I already knew in my heart, such as we are all One, etc.

A few short days after Rich's experience and mine of not see-ing him breathe, we were having a session and Rich's body suddenly went stiff again. Just as suddenly our room was filled with the most beautiful feeling of love! It was as if the entire room was overflowing with love and Yeshua was there. He said, "My child, my child" and then he proceeded to tell me things that only he could possibly know. He also helped my heart and my soul. He told me that was the rea-son the Angels were preparing Rich's body – so that He could come through to us. It was a magnificent and emotional experience for us.

Once He departed; Rich was racked with sobs due to the emotional feelings. We were both crying with the emotion of this whole experience! We have never told anyone about this because we didn't think anyone would believe it, and because it was so very personal to us.

Before this experience, I had spoken to Yeshua many times within my mind and gotten answers, the same way in which I communicate with our Creator/God. However, this was the first time that a vibratory energy such as Yeshua was able to come through in such a channeling type mode. We felt truly blessed as well as humbled by this experience.

Since that time, so many things happened in our lives, such as the Entities telling us we needed to leave the East Coast sooner than we had planned. They wanted us to leave before December 2007, or no later than the first week of December. We had originally planned on moving from New Jersey in March 2008 to the new home we purchased in the White Mountains of Arizona. We had been guided to move there. Not only did we have to sell my home in Northern, New Jersey, but we also had to sell my mother's home in Southern, New Jersey, because she was moving with us. We had to move both locations, and plan a wedding all before our move across the country —talk about pressure!

We decided to get married at The Journey Within Spiritualist Church on November 24, 2007, leave the next week, drive to Arizona and arrive on December 8, 2007. We were planning on stopping in different states and visiting some spiritual sites. The moving company was scheduled to be there on a certain date, so we were not in any hurry. However, because the Entities insisted that we "get out of Dodge" by a certain period of time, I was in a

EPILOGUE

quandary as to whether we should fly and stay in a hotel until our furniture arrived (and let the moving company take both cars), or drive ourselves to Arizona in one car.

We were told by Angels, Star and Light Beings something very important was about to happen and someone very high up would be coming to us and we should prepare. When the Entity came through, I knew immediately who it was because of the overwhelming feeling of "Home" and unconditional love that enveloped us. The voice was a bit intimidating at first because it is totally direct and knowing. He/She said to me "I AM THAT I AM, I AM THAT IS." He/She said," You have a question for me and you wanted guidance, I have come in person to give you that answer." He/She told us that we were to drive over land and not fly. There was a bit more, but it was personal. For us to hold that kind of energy was extremely difficult. If you think Yeshua's visit was a miracle, than this was a double miracle! The feelings this visit left us with were unbearable. Again, this is the first time it has been written about, or spoken about, to anyone other than ourselves. It also has never occurred again, either by Yeshua or the Creator/ God. Believe me, there have been many times I wished for either's input. However, I went back to the way I communicated with them and that is how I receive my answers. I firmly believe that they came through to let us know that it was truly them, not that we ever needed proof!

We keep being told that we have much work to do. Since we have been in the White Mountains of Arizona we have had not only Angels, Star Beings, and Light Beings coming through, but also Native American Spirit Guides. One is named White Cloud;

one is called Whole Running Bear and some with Anasazi names such as Amato and Enchu, for example.

(1/24/2009)

We have been introduced to yet another group of Entities that come from what they call the "Blue Place." We have been told that this is the place where Yeshua is from and also Rich! All this time we hadn't known where Rich originated, but we were told that we were different from one another. I was a Star Being originally from Pleiades. These "Blue Place" Entities seem to be harder for Rich to channel or bring through than the Light Beings or Star Beings. It is also harder for them to speak in our language, which makes it tougher to understand what they are trying to convey to us. Just the other night or early morning, we had a visit from another Entity called Set or Seth, and he stayed for a long time. I believe he came to more or less prepare me since his message seemed to be that my mother does not have much longer on this Physical Plane. Now, that was not how he put it. He just said, "Big One, not long here." Then he proceeded to tell me that the physical body is not important. It is the spirit that is important. He also told me not to take things hard because it is not good for me. He assured me, "I am doing for her, and make happy now."

Last night an Entity named Sam came through, and he was also from the "Blue Place."

He told me that I should be writing down all of these channelings because Rich cannot remember them. I have not gotten all of them since many of them I can't remember either.

EPILOGUE

(1/27/2009)

In the early morning hours we were told that it was time, and the book must get out to the people. Imagine my surprise when in the evening of the same day the Angels came through and asked," What was I waiting for?" When I asked, "What are you referring to?" they said that they told me it was necessary for me to take the lead and get the book out! I told them it was only that morning they had told me, and I hadn't time to do it. Once again, I was told how important it was. "The time is now." The book was meant for the people and we had a part to play. What that part is we will have to discover.

ACKNOWLEDGEMENT

We want to Thank all of the Angels, Archangels, Spirit Guides, Star Beings and other Entities that we have encountered on the path, as well as Yeshua, and Creator/God. We know that all of you will continue to be with us.

We wish to thank Bruce Moen, author of *Voyage Beyond Doubt,* and Paul Elder, author of *Eyes of an Angel.* Both of these books helped us tremendously.

We especially wish to thank Ray Brennan for editing the manuscript and Masomeh Fritz for formatting it. Ray and Masomeh are wonderful friends of ours, and the authors of *The Legacy of the Chosen One,* a unique book about a true spirit transfer. On June 8, 2009, the Book Expo of America awarded its Silver Prize for the Best New Release to Ray Brennan and Masomeh Fritz for their non-fiction book, *The Legacy of the Chosen One.* This Book Expo was held in New York City at the Javits Center for publishers, agents, writers, librarians, and book lovers. There were over 30,000 attendees.

Dee and I wholeheartedly recommend this book to everyone.

For questions or comments about our book
'*Talking With Angels*' we can be reached at
talkingwithangels.tumi@gmail.com